Me, Mike, and the Agency

How Boston's JF&CS Rescued Us
and Other Kids in Need

Ben Gordon

iUniverse, Inc.
Bloomington

Me, Mike, and the Agency
How Boston's JF&CS Rescued Us and Other Kids in Need

iUniverse books may be ordered through booksellers or by contacting:

iUniverse
1663 Liberty Drive
Bloomington, IN 47403
www.iuniverse.com
1-800-Authors (1-800-288-4677)

ISBN: 978-1-4759-3263-8 (sc)
ISBN: 978-1-4759-3265-2 (hc)
ISBN: 978-1-4759-3264-5 (ebk)

Printed in the United States of America

iUniverse rev. date: 07/19/2012

for Leonard Serkess

Introduction

Sixty years ago my brother and I came to rely upon a charitable agency for the physical and emotional support our parents could not provide. My memoir relates our family difficulties and the manner in which the agency was, or was not, able to satisfy our needs. I have tried to capture and convey my emotional responses to the circumstances in which we found ourselves. I have also considered agency policies and practice as they affected Mike and me and other children whose lives were profoundly influenced by the Jewish Family and Children's Service of Boston.

The terms "group home" and "foster care" are fearsome labels, Dickensian in character, associated as they frequently are with unthinkable historic and modern outrages. But the quality of care Mike and I received had nothing in common with these horrors. Our association with the agency began in 1950 when I was nine and Mike eight; it lasted until February, 1962. During that span we lived, together, in three group homes and two foster homes. We encountered many children whose needs were at least as demanding as ours and many adults whose responsibility it was to respond constructively to those needs. Despite significant exceptions, they did so with professionalism, sensitivity and personal care, all within a framework determined by the agency. I am indebted to the many adults whose job it was to make us whole.

I began this memoir having learned that our agency records had been lost. They had disappeared, I was told, over the many years and amidst several office moves. But one morning I received an e-mail message from Betsy Hochberg, a social worker at the agency's current office in Waltham, Massachusetts. We had stayed in touch because she never lost hope that the records might be found. They had been. "Five fat folders" were mine for the asking, a three-hour drive from my Connecticut home, and evidence that I am my brother's legal executor.

Seated at a restaurant near the agency's office, my wife and I talked at length with Betsy and Amy Johnson, also an agency social worker. Amy had read the contents of Mike's and my case files in order to redact names to protect individuals' privacy. In the process she became intimately familiar with the documents, enough to warn me that the passage of time had not reduced their power to hurt. She wanted me to be emotionally prepared for what the files contained. She explained that the standards of social work had changed since these reports had been written. Much that might be considered inappropriately value-laden and needlessly graphic today was permissible, even desirable, in reports written so long ago. I nodded my understanding of the need to approach the files circumspectly, and eagerly accepted from Amy the documents in their manila folders. Only later, seated within the quiet of a darkening evening, the files opened before me, did I truly understand what she had tried to tell me.

From the start, student and professional caseworkers scrutinized, by their supervisors, regularly prepared and dictated comprehensive and detailed reports regarding Mike's and my physical and emotional conditions and those of our parents. These reports constitute the bulk of our files. Many of them concern matters about which we could not have known then and are revelations to me today. Others correct, confirm or expand my memory. Many force me to consider matters buried by us long ago in avoidance of the pain they entailed.

The files include various additional documentation: impressions of "group workers," counselors who supervised our daily activities and formed opinions concerning our behavior and what it indicated about our emotional states; results of physical, psychological, and vocational aptitudes examinations; evidence of scholastic problems and accomplishments; correspondence with hospital personnel knowledgeable about our mother's illness; correspondence with my caseworker when I had attained the age of letter-writing; and much more evidence of life on the ground for twelve years.

In short, without the extraordinary perspective and the wealth of information these documents provide I could not have understood an enormous amount of our circumstances and our relation to the agency. I could not have written this memoir.

Of course, there were many moments and feelings I remember without the assistance of the agency files. In fact, we did our very best to conceal several of these from others as well as from ourselves. Mike preferred to talk incessantly in order to avoid confronting a disturbing issue while I simply refused to acknowledge its existence. Our personal modes of denial made the task of understanding us a challenging one and rendered us emotionally impoverished, unable to grieve even for our mother or to admit our considerable pain.

Regardless of my attempts to insulate myself from painful realities, however, I did try to understand what was happening to my family as it was happening. I would lie awake in bed in the dark listening to the muffled sounds of my parents' conversation, my body rigid with anticipation but unable to distinguish a clear stream of words that bore the meaning I sought. Sometimes Uncle Shuval would be there, smoking his cigarettes and dropping ashes upon Mama's prized maple kitchen table. His would become a third voice in these conversations, but I could understand almost nothing, particularly when those voices rose as one in volume, as they usually did.

Questions plagued me. Why were Aunt Minnie, Aunt Natalie, Uncle Louie and Aunt Lily in my home so often these days? Why was Mama behaving so strangely? Why was Daddy so quiet? What was happening? What was happening to me?

Our father and our aunts and uncles must have conspired to keep Mike and me in the dark, as on one summer afternoon when Aunt Lily gave us each a shiny quarter to spend as we liked at the local drugstore. The prospect of sitting at the soda fountain, slowly eating a "college ice" while turning on the silver stool one way, then another, was impossible to resist, but I knew, however vaguely, I was being bribed in order that understanding be kept from me.

Our relatives, of course, were attempting to protect us from the grim circumstances whose roots, they thought, children could not begin to fathom and that could only cause them pain—this despite the fact that Mike and I were directly experiencing those circumstances day in and day out and desired some measure of understanding. Looking backward, I cannot fault their good intentions. Nevertheless, I now recognize in their policy of silence and evasion a degree of condescension that left me continually anxious and burdened with the obscure knowledge that an important part of my life was being kept from me.

I had no knowledge of whose idea it was that Mike and I be taken from our mother and father, our friends, our neighborhood, our school and cared for by strangers. We were never consulted. But I do know that our parents were increasingly incapable of caring for us and that our several aunts and uncles were unwilling or unable to take us in except in small doses. And although I cannot be certain of such an eventuality, I feel there is every reason to believe that our stories in the years to come were a great deal happier than they would have been without the agency's intervention.

OUR PARENTS INSISTED THAT MIKE AND I STAY TOGETHER

"The Rabbit"

The room is high-ceilinged and lit only by a domed lamp on the ponderous wooden desk. The light glows like burnished brass against the surrounding shadow. Outside, the night is filled with fog. I remember almost nothing of how I had come to be there, only the hiss of tires on a wet street and the sweet smell of rain. A man dressed in an overcoat, his gray fedora on his knee, is my father. He is turned away from me and, leaning, speaks in whispers to the woman on the other side of the desk. Somewhere in the room must be my brother, but I cannot place him or see him at all. I sit against the wall in a large, straight-backed chair. My legs dangle from the cushioned seat as I listen to fragments of a conversation I am not meant to hear. I understand almost nothing of what is happening to me. I am still and silent and I feel very small. Suddenly I am aware that I have been holding my breath.

We are riding in a car again. It is dark. A man whose large hand I had shaken is driving. My father is not there. He had knelt and looked at us and told us that Mama was sick again but she would get better and that soon we would be home again. His face was close to mine, a large, oval face with deep downward lines from the corners of the mouth. His moustache scratched my cheek when he kissed me. I could smell his Old Spice after-shave lotion. It came in the white jar with a blue sailing ship on it. He smiled at me but his face was sad. When I hugged him his coat smelled faintly of mothballs.

There is a small, oval window in the rear. I can turn and see the red lights of cars falling away in the night. But turning makes me feel nauseous. If I lean against the wall of the car, and hold on to the looped strap that is attached above, and press my forehead against the cool window at my side I feel better. Michael sits beside me, but we do not touch. He stares straight ahead.

Morning seems so long ago and far away. From my bed I had looked up and seen its dim light pressing against the near window. Michael slept in the other bed, parallel to mine. The walls were a glossy blue, newly painted. It was a school day, and almost time to get up. My father would have gone to work at the truck garage long before and Mama would have placed breakfast for us on the kitchen table. I waited for her to come and get us up. I lay there trying to recall my dream but could not. In my chest was a feeling I could not have named then had I tried. Now I know it for what it was. It was dread.

She had been strange the last few days, as if she were not really seeing me, as if there were something just beyond me she was trying unsuccessfully to make out. As usual I had helped as she washed dishes in the sink, drying them with the dishtowel, but she had nothing to say to me. I tried to talk about Toastie and her new kittens. "Yes, Benjy." Could I play with Stevie in a little while? "Yes, Benjy." Ordinarily we would talk there about all sorts of things, but lately she was as she had been that time before when I had to call my father at work. Then Mama had gone away and Michael had stayed with Aunt Natalie, in Dorchester, and I had stayed with Aunt Marion, in Haverhill. And as I lay in bed waiting for her to get us up for school I knew she would not come.

But still I was surprised to hear the knock on the door to our apartment. I sat up and waited for another. When it came, firmly, insistently, I got out of bed and walked to the next room, my bare feet cool on the linoleum. The door was reddish and strangely grained. It opened from the living room onto a dark hall that a solitary hanging light bulb struggled to illuminate. Almost directly across was the door to the furnace room where the rats lived. Ever since I had been big enough it had been my job to empty the trash into the "incinerator". I had to lift the latch and pull open the heavy steel door, throw the garbage into the black maw, quickly slam the door and, my heart pounding, run the few steps before I could gain my apartment and my mother and safety. I ran less now, but still I trembled. I knew the nearness to me and my family of nightmare.

I opened the door and saw my mother. She was wearing her long, pale nightgown with the blue flowers. Her brow furrowed as she frowned and stared beyond me. A policeman held her wrist in his big hand. He wore a dark blue uniform and had a big badge on his chest and a flat hat. My mother's hair was long and uncombed. She had not put on the salve and thin cloth bandage for her cheek that would never heal. The wound looked raw. She stood there and gave no sign that she knew me. The policeman had a round face.

"Is this your mother?" he asked, looking down at me.

"Yes."

"She was walking on the street."

"Mama, come in," I said.

I put out my hand and she took it in hers. She came into our apartment and the policeman stood in the dim hall and looked at us, tilting his head slightly to one side, and went away. I shut the door and I led her into her bedroom and urged her to get into bed and waited until she did. I left her and went to get the ice bag from the shelf under the sink in the bathroom. It was made of a gray canvass kind of material with black stripes and it was lined with rubber. It had a metal screw top into which you could fit ice cubes and pour water. It helped my mother when she had her headaches. I filled the bag with cold water and brought it to her. She was lying in bed and took it and thanked me and put the bag on her forehead and closed her eyes. I left her there. It was time to call my father.

I sat straight up and peered through the space between the front seats as the car slowed and turned right into a driveway. Then I saw the eyes, glowing and white. Their power to remain with me through the years that have followed that evening has likely been enhanced by my fear and confusion at the time. They shone there, illuminated by the car's headlights, surrounded by the darkness at the foot of the long driveway. I would learn the next morning that they belonged to a pet rabbit in its wire hutch, but at the moment of turning into the driveway they were disembodied and fascinating.

Of the woman who had talked with our father that evening and the man who had driven us to that driveway we knew nothing. Of the man at the door to whom my brother and I were passed and who led us through the spacious hall and up the curved staircase and down another hall to the room in which we were to sleep that night we knew nothing. Lying in bed, sleep coming heavily upon me, listening to the breathing of strangers asleep in the dark room, I saw the eyes. And I vaguely understood that it would fall to me in the days and years to come to learn what they seemed to know.

Parents

Mike and I became agency wards after years of dysfunctional family life. Mama was often physically and mentally ill. She was tortured by migraine attacks that forced her to lie motionless in bed for hours. She told me that she had been a "blue baby," that something was wrong with her heart. (She would die of pericarditis, an inflammation of the heart's lining). She suffered from a painful skin condition, ultimately diagnosed as lupus *vulgaris*, that left her right cheek permanently raw, requiring daily applications of ointments and thin cotton cloths which she cut in ovals to fit the contours of her face.

There were happy times, remarkable for their occurring outside the ordinary frame of our lives, or because they were, indeed, ordinary. I cherished those moments, for instance, when Mama attended to her cheek before the bathroom mirror and talked to me. I would sit on the toilet cover and look up at her as we discussed the people and events of my world. I knew in those moments that she loved me. I felt, in fact, that I was her favorite because Mike did not share in these private conversations. Besides, hadn't I been born on Mama's birthday? Hadn't she sung to me "You were meant for me, I was meant for you . . ." and to Mike only "You made me love you, I didn't want to do it . . . ?" I needed my mother's love and I found its clear expression in intimate times like these.

I remember, in particular, a special time with Mama and Mike at Boston's Museum of Fine Arts. In anticipation of a great day I brought my Brownie box camera and still have a photograph I took in front of the museum. It is of Mama and Mike standing on the museum's frozen lawn. Behind them is the statue of the Indian chief mounted on his horse, arms spread wide, Mama explained, in token of his complete openness to the Great Spirit.

It is cold: Mike wears a bulky coat, a hat and earmuffs. Mama wears gloves and a coat with fur trim down its front and along its hem. She holds a paper bag that must have been heavy or awkward to carry judging from the manner in which she clutches it to her chest. She is smiling, her head turned slightly to her right (always to her right, exposing her unscarred left cheek to the camera).

In that bag were bowls, shiny dark green and brown, each with a single, tubular handle that protruded from its side. Sitting at the counter of a steamy diner, the three of us had slurped with relish the hot pea soup served to us in those bowls. What fun it was when Mama asked the counter man if she might buy four of those bowls! How happy we were when he said yes! Wouldn't Daddy be surprised! And we could all sit down in our own kitchen and eat from those bowls soup that Mama had made and remember our trip to the museum and the Indian chief!

In such small things we discovered much happiness.

IT WAS IMPORTANT TO OUR DAD
THAT WE KNEW HE LOVED US

"Laundry"

I sat on the toilet seat cover and watched Mama wash the soiled clothes in the bathtub. She wore her housedress, the one with the pink flowers. I had watched her kneel on the white tiled floor to soak them, rub them hard on the washboard with the bar of yellow soap, rinse them beneath the tub's spigot, and wring them into tight twists of fabric. Now she was piling the multi-colored pieces into the straw basket with the big handles and the red stitching.

Through the open window above the tub I could see the driveway that ran along the building's brick side and beyond that the empty lot illuminated by summer afternoon sunshine. I could hear Artie and Steve and Mike yelling delightedly as they played punchball. But I had no intention of joining them that day. I sat up straighter as I watched Mama stand, place her hands on the small of her back, then raise them to the ceiling and stretch from her waist. I saw the perspiration that covered the back of her neck, and when she turned to look down at me I saw it glisten on her forehead and upper lip.

She smiled.

"Benjy, why don't you go outside and play with your friends?"

"No, Mama, I want to help you with the laundry."

"But it's such a nice day."

"No, Mama."

She sighed and bent to kiss my upturned face.

"Alright, then. Hold onto a handle."

The clotheslines were hung in a central courtyard enclosed by the walls of two apartment buildings. Most were high, extending from windowsills four stories above ground level. Looking up, I saw that Mrs. Cohen had already hung out her laundry. The pieces were draped like gay flags from a line that stretched from her window on the second floor to a pulley on the opposite wall. Beyond them were tiers of windows, empty lines and a square of pale blue sky.

Moving clumsily, Mama and I carried our basket through the dark antechamber to our apartment, past the coal storage room, into the main hallway, through a narrow door on the left and into the cool air of the concrete-gray courtyard. Sometimes Mama let me carry the basket all by myself, but today it was too heavy for that and we each held a handle.

Mama took two wooden clothespins from the striped cotton sack that hung by a thin metal hook from our line and gave them to me.

"Here. You are getting so big you can reach the line in the middle. You can hang the laundry there. I will hang things on the ends."

First, I selected a white pillowcase. Mama had taught me how to shake it out and hang it from its corners. I worked carefully, stretching my body and my arms to secure both the clothespins and the pillowcase they held to the line. I smiled when I had done so, for I knew I had hung it correctly and that Mama would be proud of me.

9

"Look, Mama."

"That's perfect, dear. You are a smart boy and getting to be so grown-up. What will you hang up next?"

Soon all the laundry was hanging from the line. I looked at it and was glad.

"Look, Mama. It's so pretty."

"Yes, Benjy, it is."

I picked up the empty basket and we walked to the apartment.

"Thank you, Benjy. You did a good job. Will you help me take the laundry down when it's dry?"

"Yes, Mama, I will."

Mike was excited when he came in from play.

"You shoulda seen it, Mama. I hit the ball over everything, way in the bushes."

Mama brought two glasses of milk to us, seated by the window at the kitchen table.

"You're getting to be so strong, Mikey," Mama said.

I looked down at my hands, quietly folded in my lap, and smiled. I thought I knew something that my brother did not.

This is the way I like to remember my mother, as a calm, caring, and happy person whom I loved without qualification. But I have come to realize that memory captures only part of the truth. It is endlessly selective and wants to protect or to shape its subject, as if it were a malleable work in progress on the potter's wheel.

If I were to accept even part of what my wife tells me whenever one of us raises the issue I would have to agree that to an advanced stage in writing the first draft of this memoir I did not dare to explore the whole truth of my relationship with my mother. I would have to admit that the relationship was more complex than I had allowed myself to believe, even, at times, frightening. I would have to acknowledge my highly selective memory, my ability to conveniently forget much of my childhood experience, and my idealization of my mother, whose frequently negative presence continues to affect my behavior many years after her death.

Mama was often unable to act as I prefer to remember her: to sing, to talk, to care for us, to do all those things that mamas do. Mike and I learned early to shift for ourselves at these times, careful not to speak too loudly so not to disturb her, finding our own food on the sparsely provisioned shelves of the fridge and the kitchen cabinets, preparing our own peanut butter sandwiches to take each day as lunch to school, returning home to the ominous silence that prevailed in the rooms of our apartment, silence that carried with it the possibility that we had in some way failed to meet her exacting standards.

MAMA WAS PROUD OF HER SONS

Mama was occasionally hospitalized in the psychiatric ward of the Boston State Hospital, for she became subject to "breakdowns," days when she behaved strangely and left Mike and me in a constant state of apprehension. She would wander as if in a trance about our little apartment, unseeing, unresponsive, inhabiting her own peculiar world. At these times she would shout to no one—or to everyone—her refusal to perform her usual housekeeping tasks. Mumbling, and dressed only in a nightgown, her long brown hair tangled and matted, she would sometimes leave the apartment to wander upon the sidewalks of our Roxbury neighborhood preaching the New Testament.

Our father seemed to know only two responses to her behavior. He would shout at her, futilely commanding her to make the beds, to cook, to clean, to take care of Mike and me. Failing in that, he would flee. When he left for Boston's North Terminal truck garage, where he worked as a dispatcher and where he found sanctuary from his domestic ordeal, he would instruct me as the oldest to call him if Mama started "talking funny" and things got out of hand. He would then promise to be home before we went to bed and advise us to "be good boys." In short, we were on our own and never knew what to expect from one day to the next.

If, as I believe, our father did nothing to effectively deal with this situation in the hope that it would go away on its own, circumstances would soon demonstrate that it would not. Like Mike and me, he had become expert at using denial as a shield with which to protect himself against circumstances he could not control. He must have been terrified by the dissolution of his family and the emergence of another wife than he had known. His own limitations rendered him incapable of protecting Mike and me from the realities it was our lot to experience. Over the years I have worked hard to see my father in a kinder light than that which cast such shadows upon Mike's and my childhoods. I wanted to make clear to myself that our father's place there wasn't all brown and sour like the whiskey he drank, to airbrush his image in the service of my own powerful denial.

"The Shirt"

Mama said it was a present from Mike and me even though we didn't have any money and she bought it herself in the men's department of Filenes and all we did was watch. It is the thought that counts, she said. The lady behind the counter put it in a box and wrapped it in shiny red paper and she asked us if we wanted her to tie it with a ribbon and we said yes, please.

I carried the bag on the train ride to Egleston Square and Mike carried it to our streetcar stop on Seaver Street and Mama carried it into the apartment in case Daddy was home already from work because we wanted it to be a surprise and it was hard to wait until tomorrow when it would be Father's Day and he could unwrap it but we did. The next day after breakfast before we got changed to go to the baseball game he sat in his chair in the living room and we gave it to him and he was surprised and he unwrapped it and opened the box and looked at it and unfolded it and smiled and held it up to show Mama and he said it was great and that he loved the color and that he would even wear it today at the baseball park.

It was bright yellow and there were little bunches of brown lines crossing each other all over and it had short sleeves and white buttons and it looked bran new, which it was, of course, and just before we left the apartment he went into his bedroom and he put it on and I liked to look at him dressed in it because he was my dad and he was wearing the shirt Mike and I gave him for Father's Day.

Mama held the door open as we left. We were early because Daddy said it was fun to watch batting practice. Mama kissed us and said she wanted her men to have a good time. We said we would. We waited at the streetcar stop and other men came with their sons and some girls even came and I looked around for kids I knew but didn't see any but I knew that some of them would be at the game with their dads. After the streetcar ride we got on the trolley to Massachusetts Avenue and we walked from there over the Muddy River to Fenway Park.

Daddy held our hands as we walked through the crowd near the gate that was for the bleachers. We could know where he was because his shirt was so bright and he was tall but I was glad that he held my hand anyway. He bought the tickets from a man in a kind of cage and we walked to the gate and he gave the tickets to another man who tore them up and gave one part back to our dad. He said they were rain checks and I thought that was funny because it was so sunny. It was very crowded and we needed to squeeze in between people but it was exciting to know that soon we would be there.

Inside it was cool and shady and people were buying things like hats and hot dogs and popcorn and it smelled nice, like butter. We went up the ramp to the long wooden benches and the sunny space and the green field and the blue sky and the players. The ones wearing gray uniforms were there and Daddy said that meant that they were the visitors and that the Red Sox would be coming out of their dugout soon for practice and they would have white uniforms. We picked a bench right near the Red Sox bullpen where the pitchers stayed during the game and we could watch them practice if the manager wanted them to play. Daddy bought us popcorn and tonic and he bought a big cup of beer

15

and we watched the people come into the bleachers and sit on the benches. Mike sat on one side of our dad and I sat on the other and we watched batting practice and the players throwing the balls and catching them and we waited for the game to start.

When the Red Sox came on the field everyone cheered and we cheered after the man sang the song and we cheered after the Red Sox scored a run or caught the ball. Daddy explained lots of things to us and said we were really good fans and that he was proud of us and he thanked us again for his new shirt.

After the game we stayed on our bench and waited for the people to leave until the bleachers were almost empty. The sun made long shadows on the grass and everything was soft like when you stroke a cat. But when Daddy asked us if we would like to have supper in a restaurant we both said yes and we left, too.

In the restaurant you had to pick up a tray and silverware and walk in a line and tell the man behind the counter what you wanted. I told him that I wanted Salisbury Steak and mashed potatoes and peas and a glass of milk and Daddy carried my tray and Mike's tray and we sat in seats across from him and while we ate we talked about the game and Ted Williams and Bobby Doerr and the other players. I had chocolate pudding with whipped cream for dessert and I thanked my dad for buying it. Mike had the same thing and he thanked Daddy, too. When we left it was almost dark outside.

When we got home we sat at the kitchen table and Mama asked us who won the game and what we had for supper and if we had a good time. We said we did and told her about the restaurant and about the home run Ted Williams hit and about how we stayed in the park so long and how pretty it was and then it was time for bed.

After we washed our face and hands and brushed our teeth and got our pajamas on we got into bed and read our comic books and Mama came in and kissed us goodnight and then Daddy came in and he was still wearing his yellow shirt and he kissed us goodnight and said that he had a wonderful day with us and we said we did too and then he turned off the light.

NEW SUITS FOR PASSOVER BRING OUT THE HAM IN US

My memories of the good times with our dad are keen but even the baseball idyll now seems tainted by his addiction to alcohol. We would walk to Fenway from the trolley stop on Mass. Ave., always stopping by a particular storefront before we reached the Muddy River. Telling us he would not be long, he would go in, leaving Mike and me to wait on the sidewalk until he emerged. Although I feel a natural sympathy for him in his difficult circumstances, I know that at the root of our domestic ordeal was his inability to honestly confront the realities of his situation, his finding solace in drink, and his evasion of responsibility for his wife's and his children's welfare.

Early in our relationship with the agency our caseworker, Sylvia Chayet, registered her "surprise" to learn of our father's "casual attitude toward his wife's condition and his apparent unwillingness to do anything about it." She discussed the matter with her supervisor and visited my father at the garage where he worked "in order to further attempt to explain to him the need for his wife to resume her treatment, her incapability to assume full responsibility for the boys in her present situation, and his responsibility as a father to attempt to formulate adequate plans to meet the situation."

"Quite complacent," she continued, and satisfied with declarations like 'She is alright with the boys, she takes good care of them' and 'Everything will be alright,'" our father consistently demonstrated his inability to come to grips with our family's deterioration. As another caseworker observed, he possessed no understanding of the psychic stress this situation imposed on us. Such constant evasion and lack of understanding, of course, allowed him to do as little as possible in response.

One bothersome but symptomatic area of our father's relationship with the agency was his frequent neglect of the agreement he had made to contribute a nominal sum of money toward the cost of our care, taking into account the ordinary demands upon his salary.

Administering the various arms of the agency was an expensive proposition, made possible by the largesse of the Associated Jewish Philanthropies (now the Combined Jewish Philanthropies) and the agency's own financial resources. Parental contributions were unlikely to make a dent in these costs but they emblemized the parents' commitment to their child's welfare even when the child was beyond their control. The issue was raised during my father's second interview with an agency caseworker. Here is that entry:

> In the initial survey of payments to the agency, Mr. G. agreed that at this time he could handle $15 per wk. for the two boys. This amount was arrived at after evaluation of the man's salary of $60 per wk., which was to be used for maintaining the present apartment, $40 per mo. for utilities, 3 meals a day on the outside, carfare and incidentals. Mr. G claims that he is compelled to pay off large medical bills which his wife accumulated. The exact amount of these bills should be determined in the near future, both for the reality of the statement and for the purpose of reaching the point of having Mr. G. pay $10 per wk. for each boy. This was discussed with Mr. G. by worker as he felt he could not pay this amount at present.

Over the years of his relationship with the agency, our father sometimes paid the agreed-upon sum, often neglected to pay anything for long periods, almost always paid less than the agency felt was possible, given the fact made clear to him that he would have to expend more than the stipulated amount in support of his boys were they living at home. As one caseworker facetiously phrased the matter when assured by my father that he would resume long-neglected payments for Mike and me, "Evidently, Mr. G. can make promises, then fail to meet them." Another caseworker remarked that our father was likely to be "somewhat vague" and "evasive" when the issue of promised payments was raised. Put another way, though he loved us by his standards, and visited us with regularity wherever we lived, our father was weak in our support—as the agency was strong in our defense.

After our mother's death, on the occasions of our Sunday visits to the Seaver Street apartment, our father would sit in the dilapidated armchair in the living room (our mother had covered its frayed arms with doilies) and speak to us of how unfortunate his life had been. He spoke of the promise he had felt as a high school graduate, the hard work he had put in to support his family, all of its having come to nothing, and the difficulties he had endured in his marriage. By then I understood that his personal failures had played a large part in his own and the family's disintegration. He had been a feared disciplinarian when we were children, meting out punishment upon his return from work with his bare hand on our naked bottoms when he received a bad report from our mother regarding our behavior that day. But now I understood him to be a broken and disappointed man dependent upon whiskey. In fact, he sometimes commissioned me to walk down Humboldt Avenue to the drugstore and exchange a bill with the smiling man in back for a bottle in a brown paper bag: his "medicine". I felt then that there was something sinister about these errands but did not understand their relationship to the dissolution of our family.

Mike and I needed a father upon whom we could rely. Although ours worked hard to provide for his family, surely his denial, his passivity, and his drinking contributed heavily to his wife's psychosis and his children's loss of a viable family life. Our adult determination to be responsible fathers was formed by our experiences of a family life in which we could count on nothing. It was also enhanced by the role models we found in some of the housefathers hired by the agency to be our surrogate dads. In this capacity, Frank O'Rourke was my Shane.

Frank was tall and handsome and he taught us the things fathers teach their sons: how to hang up your pants so they keep their crease; to throw to the cutoff man rather than try for the man racing home, even if you do think (as I did) your arm is as good as Jimmy Piersall's; to soften your beard with hot water before applying the shaving cream (Gerry and Bobby already shaved and the rest of us longed for the blessed event). Frank was willing to share himself even in intimate matters. He was willing, for example, to discuss the large brown warts that grew on his hands and the process required to burn them off. He was there for us, a steady presence whom we all admired and loved. A photograph of Frank teaching chess to several of us thirteen and fourteen-year-olds clustered about him in the Bradshaw House living room is mute testimony to the strength of that bond.

Conversely, while Mike and I gained a temporary father in this manner, my own father's weakness for alcohol cost him one of his sons. Mike never saw him again after he collapsed upon the living room's scarred linoleum and lost control of his bowels during one of our regular Sunday visits. Turning from my father and just before the apartment door slammed shut, I saw my brother, already in the dark hall: his wide eyes stay with me.

Our father was drinking heavily and eating poorly at that time, so that he was severely undernourished when he entered the hospital to which he had been brought by the police after my telephone call. Mike insisted "over and over" in interviews with Herman Steingraph, our caseworker then, that he wanted to wash his hands completely of his father and that he was not going to visit his father at Boston City Hospital or anywhere else. When Steingraph suggested that his resolve might "bounce back on him" in the form of guilt later on, Mike replied that "he was going to take his chances with his feelings."

Mike's and my relationship with our father had been declining for years. One occasion before his collapse now seems an ironic benchmark in that process. The previous spring he was too drunk even to keep his appointment with us to meet at Fenway

Park and share a game. He left Mike and me to wait and worry in the afternoon sunshine by the bleachers gate. Mike and I never discussed this instance or the larger horror, neither during the three years before our father's death, nor during the many subsequent years before Mike's own.

I know my father loved me in his way. But he didn't know how to do a good job at being a father nor did he possess the necessary strength to cope with his bleak circumstances. As I grew older I felt increasingly sorry for him and still do. Nevertheless, and despite the squeeze of guilt that accompanies my admission, I have sometimes wondered what led me to maintain with him so threadbare a relationship. After all, it was I who cleaned up the mess.

MIKE SITS NEXT TO FRANK, DANNY NEXT TO MIKE, I AM
STANDING AND GERRY LOOKS OVER HIS SHOULDER.

Our parents' first association with the agency destined to play so large a role in our lives was a cry for help in June of 1944. At ages two and three Mike and I were being cared for by our aunts while Mama was hospitalized for treatment of her face, a condition initially diagnosed as tuberculosis of the skin. But she did not have confidence in the quality of her sisters' care and wanted the agency to find a housekeeper who could care for us at home. By August the agency's efforts to do so had failed, Mama returned from the hospital and the case was closed.

A year and a half later Mama called the agency to inquire again about a housekeeper. Mike and I had the "grippe" and she had severed the tendon of her right hand by breaking and crushing a glass. Her hand was useless and she was unable to properly care for us. This time the agency managed to find a housekeeper and sent a caseworker to our apartment.

The following is an excerpt from the caseworker's report of her interview with our mother at this time. In addition to its guarded reference to "the implications" of her accident, it suggests our mother's psychiatric problems for it captures the brittle quality of her demeanor and the domineering and compulsive nature of her speech. Without the understanding we sought, Mike and I nevertheless knew these to be characteristic of her behavior when she was falling prey to her dementia or still under its spell.

> Mrs. G.'s sister, Miss Lilian Goldberg, opened the door and showed me into the bedroom where Mrs. G. was in bed. Miss Goldberg placed me so that I could see Mrs. G.'s right cheek, which was covered by a compress. During the interview, Miss Goldberg was present. Mrs. G. repeated her request for a housekeeper, saying that her sister had taken off time to assist her, but could not do it because she had to depend upon the money she earns. Moreover, her sister has to take care of their mother, who has a heart condition. She explained how she crushed

the glass in her hand like an eggshell. She was nervous because of the children's sickness . . . (My impression was that the injury was not quite so accidental). She is now unable to do even the lightest kind of housework and will be so incapacitated for at least two months. She is glad that the children are better. She cannot move her hand and therefore cannot button the children's clothes or put them to bed. That is the reason why she needs a housekeeper, also to give the children food.

What she said to me was said in a very monotonous way. She spoke very fast and almost systematically as though she had told that story of her sickness and the accident a hundred times. It was my impression that she spoke that way to cover up, though I am not sure what she wants to cover up—whether it is the emotions or the implications of the accident.

She then repeated that her children are better and I could go and see them. I then went to the bedroom where the boys are. Both of them are fair boys, lying in bed very quietly and looking at picture books. They were about to paint, but did not have pencils, so I gave them two pencils. I was too short a time in the room to have very much of an impression of the boys, but I can see one thing, that they did not seem to be naughty when I was in the apartment. They could not be heard in the bedroom where I was before.

Although the housekeeper secured by the agency did not work out, our mother organized enough care for us from a high school girl and a visiting nurse. Despite the nurse's and our Aunt Lily's judgment that our mother was "disorganized" and incapable of keeping house, she wanted nothing more from the agency and this case, too, was closed.

Today I am certain that the reason for the silence in our bedroom during the caseworker's visit was our listening anxiously to the conversation in our parents' bedroom. We knew the warning signs and understood that there was cause for discomfort, if not alarm.

Consider the cramped conditions in our small apartment and my mother's account of the accident to her hand, breaking and crushing the glass "like an eggshell." In her report the caseworker suggests that there was more to the incident than my mother was admitting, that the injury was "not quite so accidental." Was she correct? Had our mother been enraged when she ground the shards of glass into her palm? Even with the printed record before me I conveniently chose the coward's way while writing the first draft of my memoir and neither remembered nor dealt with the incident or its implications for our relationship. Whom or what was I protecting?

Had I been there? Had I, in some childish way (I was only four years old), considered myself responsible for her hysteria and self-mutilation? What must the moment have been like? There must have been a lot of blood. It must have spurted onto the floor of our kitchen, onto the fridge itself . . . Had she gone to the fridge exasperated by Mike's and my unruly behavior, perhaps cooped up during a rainy day in our dark apartment, gone to get us each a glass of milk, trying to calm us down, to sit us down at the table, losing control of the situation, out of her mind with the desire to punish us, to punish herself for the life she was forced to lead, for her life in the dingy apartment she hated?

I have often thought, simplistically, I admit, that the real world my mother inhabited was so disappointing that her only option was to leave it in madness. Her many brothers and sisters, all second generation Americans, had managed with their families to move up and out of their run-down neighborhoods while her reality remained a basement apartment in a declining neighborhood complete with knocking pipes and rats who infested the adjacent coal furnace room and made occasional visits to our apartment. While my conceit is pure conjecture, I think she must have blamed her husband and children for her circumstances.

My mother's father, Herman Goldberg, from Riga, Latvia, had been a jeweler and a collector of books and prints. One of the latter claimed an incongruous place of honor in the living room of our apartment. It was of Othello delighting the Venetian aristocracy with his heroic tales, a florid image I loved to contemplate. That print, several books with my mother's personal nameplate affixed to their inner covers, a set of encyclopedias, and my mother's mahogany hope chest, adornments of our shabby living quarters, represented a much-desired environment of cultural and economic attainment never to be realized by my mother, and I believe the consequences of that failure made her mad.

Agency caseworkers who met her were struck by her "compulsive" and "pathetic" attempts to be recognized as a sophisticated woman. "She tried to be ingratiating and is excessively polite," one remarked. "She attempts to give the impression of a well-cultured person and carefully chooses her vocabulary . . . Mrs. G. succeeds, however, only in giving the impression that she is trying too hard. I feel she is under a strain and not well."

My frequent experience of that strain as it was revealed in her speech and behavior, in her troubled interaction with Mike and me, allows me now, if I am honest with myself, to understand something of the burden Mama's illness placed on my shoulders. She would have made me feel responsible for her harming herself. She would have lectured me in the bathroom as I helped her bandage her bloody hand with a roll of gauze and white adhesive tape. She would have reminded me of my neglected task to monitor and correct the conduct of my younger brother. She would have condemned, in an imperious tone of voice that brooked no disagreement, my own imperfections and, yes, she would have made it clear that I could expect a spanking when my father came home. No amount of my pleading—"Have we been good today, Mama? Have we?"—would prevent that.

How much of the goody-goody, so-mature-for-his-age character often ascribed to me by my agency houseparents had its roots in my relationship with a mother capable of punishing me in ways far more painful than the spankings my father administered with his hand to my bare bottom? How much of my adult conscientiousness stems from my feelings of guilt and my need to be better than I was as a child? Our case records indicate that from the beginning of our relationship with the agency our caseworkers were concerned that because of our mother's "authoritative and exacting attitude she has a domineering effect on [her sons] which may be harmful to them in their future development."

Remembered honestly, our mother ground dangerous matter into our minds just as she ground those slivers of glass into her hand. What did it matter that she was ill, as we knew by then that she was? We had little capacity to empathize with her, to understand the strain her situation imposed on her and on us. Regardless of my attempts to make her feel better when her illness took possession of her, I lived with my brother in terror and without a clue as to what to do about it.

I readily understand how my wife might ascribe my knee-jerk response to want to make things right when she is upset or tired or not feeling well to my having been scared to death of these facts of my childhood. "I am not your mother," Suzanne tells me, but too often I act in this regard as if she were.

Despite our father's and our denial of the truth that things were certainly out of control, there was no evading the severity of circumstances in our household when a telephone call at 4:30 p.m. on September 15, 1950, in essence began our lengthy association with the agency. The call was taken by Beatrice Wajdyk Carter, then Director of Children's Service at the agency and destined to play a significant role in this memoir. Here, dictated three days later, is her report regarding that call and its immediate sequel.

Telephone call from [Mrs. Cohen] who said that she was speaking on behalf of a neighbor, Mr. Gordon. She told me that Mr. Gordon was too disturbed to talk on the phone as his wife at that time was being interviewed by a psychiatrist from the State Hospital, and he just signed commitment papers. She said that two boys were completely without care, that none of their neighbors or relatives were in a position of helping. She asked that we send a housekeeper that night. I told her that that would be impossible, but that I would see the father and children if they wanted to come any time that evening. Mr. Gordon and the two boys in office at 9. Mr. Gordon was still deeply disturbed. This is the third commitment of his wife. He said that his wife became engrossed in world affairs and then began to read the Bible assiduously. She procured a New Testament and began to plead with her husband and others to please believe in Jesus if they loved her. No reassurance or explanations penetrated her illness and finally a private physician arranged for commitment. Both boys are without care. The father is a foreman mechanic in a large garage. He rises at 5:30, works twelve hours each day, and comes home too late to know what is happening to the two boys. Mrs. Gordon is a highly educated woman. She completed college, knows all the classics. Mr. Gordon seemed very proud of this, was always "above him," but their life together had been harmonious and happy. He cannot account for her mental illness nor give any definite period of onset of difficulties. Mrs. Gordon always had been a good mother, except where her illness becomes too overwhelming, at which time both boys are sadly neglected.

At this time Mr. Gordon did not know what to do with the children, and I suggested immediate placement at the Study Home, to which he agreed with great relief. The boys are homely but exceedingly appealing and apparently well mannered. There have been previous separations from the mother and father, but no agency placement as far as I could determine. During previous illness of Mrs. Gordon, relatives usually provided shelter for the children in separate homes. Mr. Gordon was far too involved in his own pain to face any planning ahead. I therefore limited my activity to the purpose of immediate placement.

Telephoned Mr. Serkess, who called for the children.

By midnight Mike and I had arrived at the agency's study home in Brighton and were on our way to bed.

Family Ties

Mike and I soon learned that it was Leonard Serkess—"Mr. Serkess" to the twenty boys and girls who lived together in the home and for whom he was responsible—who responded to Beatrice Carter's telephone call and drove us that dark night to the big house after our family circumstances had reached their breaking point. The year before, while studying for his master's degree in social work, he had been hired by the agency to be a housefather in the "study home." He remained until 1958, having by then become director of three homes, in Brighton, Newton and Dorchester. He hired and fired staff, developed and managed the budget, and supervised a program that he believed realized the agency's purpose as it was stated in its by-laws: "To provide care for those Jewish children of Boston who are deprived of a normal family life, such care to be given in accordance with the best standards of modern child welfare . . ."

Those "best standards" were defined by the agency's director, Dora Margolis, and Carter, her second in command. The two were indispensable to the agency's efforts to meet its wards' material and emotional needs. This was certainly the unreserved opinion of Bernie Schneider, then the agency's comptroller, and Serkess as expressed in a 1995 interview conducted by agency social worker Ellen Fishman:

Schneider: These two were very instrumental in helping these kids. They were wonderful.

Serkess: They were wonderful people, and I think that without their concern . . . they really nurtured these kids, they worried as if they were their own children, and whatever progress [the children] made can be attributed to them . . .

Schneider: Mrs. Carter and Miss Margolis, they really did the job well. I think their primary thrust of concern was the families, of course, but especially with the children. When it came to budget time, and certain kids had to go to [private schools for troubled children], she would budget for them. We would sit at this meeting, and they would say that it cost too much money . . . and she said, "I don't care. These kids need the care, and I am going to send them regardless of whether you give me the money or not." And she did, too.

Serkess: The budget reality was of little concern to Dora Margolis. I remember we needed a nurse. She went to the Beth Israel Hospital, took a nurse, and gave her room and board at [the Brighton Home] . . . She was very clever in maneuvering, but I could remember many nights until 12 or 1 at night that she would be on the phone calling up people and getting money. You remember those nights?

Schneider: She just went ahead and said, "I don't care! You have to see him tomorrow!" And sure enough, the doctor saw him.

Serkess: Whoever it was, she was very, very clever, and very aggressive. But it was for the children.

Central to the framework of policies within which these men worked was the assurance stated in the agency's by-laws that each child served by the agency and his parents be guaranteed modern, efficient, individualized casework service. The first issue requiring steady application of this principle to the problems Mike and I and our parents faced came to the fore immediately after our arrival, so to speak, on the agency's doorstep.

Our mother had been committed twice to a psychiatric hospital before Mike and I were taken to the study home. Her third hospitalization lasted for five weeks. Our case files reveal that soon after her release she expressed to our caseworker her desire to bring us home quickly. Only the fact that she was "desperately tired all the time," she said, explained why she did not immediately take us from the Home. Our caseworker, Sylvia Chayet, assured her that we were being well cared for, and while this seemed to put her at ease she was still looking forward to our speedy return to our Roxbury apartment. Both agreed, however, that this should happen only when she was better.

That accord was brief. Two weeks later our mother expressed "great anxiety" regarding Mike and me and required Chayet's multiple assurances that we would not be moved from Brighton to a foster home without her consent. A week later, still feeling exhausted, she planned to be ready soon for our return. "Her husband," she said, "misses them very much as he is strongly attached to them and would want to take them home next Sun." Although she felt they should wait a while longer, and although "worker encourages her in this attitude," three days later she called to announce that she was perfectly capable of caring for us. She and our father insisted that we be returned to our home that weekend.

Chayet talked with a Boston State Hospital social worker who informed her that upon our mother's release it was understood that she required a long rest before assuming a mother's responsibilities. Informed of our parents' demand, her doctor thought it was a bad idea. Chayet arranged for the doctor's re-evaluation of our mother's mental state "to help us if possible to maintain our stand in the situation." Her considered opinion was "that this woman is not able now to take responsibility for the care of her two young boys."

As it turned out, an influential doctor argued that our return home might be therapeutic for our mother. In view of that attitude and her persistence, the agency concluded that the wisest plan would be to allow our mother to take us home for the Christmas vacation and during this time to work with her toward accepting the idea of returning us to the Home for a further stay. But the trauma associated with taking us again from our parents so soon now seemed to the agency an unacceptable option. The best course of action, it appeared, would be to work with parents and children in their own home. Once our parents understood that, for the welfare of the other children, our transfer would necessarily occur at the agency's Boston office, and not at the home, as they wished, the transfer was made, "both boys with their luggage packed in cartons" having been brought to the agency's office in Boston's West End.

An uneasy relationship existed between our parents and the agency for the next three months. It was punctuated by Chayet's house visits; by her supervisor's visit to our father at work; by our mother's occasionally disoriented behavior (speaking on the phone to Chayet, for instance, she heard a fire engine and insisted that the study home was burning); by our father's refusal to leave work during these periods or to acknowledge any realistic assessment of her condition or the possibility that we needed another's care; and by the ultimate agency decision to abandon further attempts to press our parents on this matter, as they might "present a threatening factor to Mrs. G . . . and may serve to precipitate her symptoms."

Less than two months later our mother was again committed to the Boston State Hospital. Our father called the agency to inform them "in an agitated manner" that his wife had been picked up by police that morning "wandering about the street partly unclothed.

When he arrived at police station she attacked him by hitting him forcibly in the face." He was calling to request that the agency resume responsibility for Mike and me.

Later that day our father brought us to the agency office. "He appeared to be quite saddened and bewildered in his acceptance of his wife's situation," Chayet reported, "but maintains a rather passive attitude in regard to his role in planning for her or for the boys. He readily consents to supervisor's suggestion that in future closer cooperation on his part with agency planning would be more helpful."

The prospect of Mike's and my returning to our home would surface many times again, and within the next two years we would visit with our parents during holidays and be visited by one or both of them on weekends. But this experience had forced upon our parents their acceptance of two realities: as long as our mother's health remained fragile she could not assume primary care for us; and their neglect of agency planning for Mike and me could only hurt us.

Mike and I sat quietly in the waiting room while arrangements between our father and the agency were completed. As soon as they were Chayet took us by subway and trolley to the Brighton home. Later she remarked in her report that we appeared to be "not visibly affected" by all we had experienced. Maintaining that appearance would become characteristic behavior throughout our years with the agency.

> They have with them a bundle of clothing which appears to be hastily put together and consists of such items as pants, jackets, pajamas, etc. and also a small pile of comic books. Both boys seem friendly and M. strives to be quite outgoing and assertive while Benjamin seems more reserved and sensible in his remarks. Mr. G. kisses both boys quite devotedly and states that he will visit

them on Sunday. The boys are not at all disturbed by his departure and seem prepared and eager to start for S.H. When it is suggested that M. help in carrying items by taking the comic books he responds that it is B. who reads them and is not willing to do so. He also complains that he is tired during walk to subway and eager to have his supper. He remains talkative during whole trip and enjoys making observations through window during bus ride. B., on the other hand, although very calm and considerate in his behavior toward his brother, maintains a rather reflective expression and remains quiet when spoken to. He asks about there being any new children at the S.H. Both boys appear relieved upon arriving at S.H. but a bit shy upon entering. They are warmly greeted by housefather and the other children eagerly surround them. They are immediately seated at the supper table and appear to be calm and content. As the others have already finished eating they remain at the table alone. Worker notes that there is no bread left on table and when she inquires if she should get them some B. replies that they don't need any but M. adds that he would like some. Worker leaves them to join the children after stating that she will visit them the following week.

I marvel at our good fortune in those circumstances. Although our parents and relatives could not or would not take care of us, we were caringly treated in a stable environment while our needs were sensitively monitored and satisfied. If we seemed unfazed by our recent experience, no worker at the agency would have considered accepting that impression at face value. Plans were soon afoot for our psychological testing. In preparation for that, Chayet wrote to Dr. Henry Platt, a clinical psychologist retained by the agency, informing him of our "frequently broken home within the past year," our "observance of and reactions to [our] mother's progressively disoriented behavior," and her own assumption that these experiences "have affected [Mike and me] in some manner." The agency was "interested in learning to what extent this has been true and how it is influencing [their] present and possible future functioning."

Any extensive planning on our behalf presumed that at present there was no possibility our family could function as a cohesive unit consistent with Mike's and my welfare. It was not enough that during our mother's periods of dementia Mike and I were strikingly self-reliant, getting up ourselves, washing and dressing, preparing our meals, and going off to school, all in our father's absence. The agency's by-laws make clear its dedication to the preservation of normal family life:

> Our primary interest is in the prevention of breakdown of the family, in strengthening family ties and in maintaining sound standards of normal family living. Our desire is to preserve the unity of the family and the integrity of the home for children at all times. When removal from the home is found essential to safeguard the security, growth and development of the child, the JFCS in furnishing the child with protection carries concomitant responsibility for the rehabilitation of the family home whenever possible.

The agency insisted that Mike and I not live at home for as long as our parents were incapable of resuming their responsibilities to us. Our father agreed to this essential condition soon after our re-admittance to the study home in April,1951: He "assures Worker that he will not make the same mistake as he did last time by insisting that the children be returned to [his wife] before she was actually ready to accept them. She is also aware of this."

Mike and I understood that we were to remain in the study home until our mother was well enough to care for us. Anything other than that, we knew, was unacceptable to the grownups.

Consequently, we were on the alert for signs of her wellness. "At worker's suggestions that mother seems to be feeling much better," Chayet remarked, "Benjamin brings out that they like it all right at the Study Home but will like better to go home when their mother is able to take care of them . . . He also notes that when his mother goes for next B[oston] S[tate] H[ospital] appointment she will inquire about how soon she can take them home."

Another time, Mike and I appeared to believe our mother was ready and able to care for us and we were eager to leave the study home: "The boys . . . after having discussed with their parents their plans for coming home, seemed somewhat more restless now and quite anxious to get home."

As a result of our mother's apparently improved health and her visits to us in Brighton, we had "become ambivalent about [our] present setting" and thought our homecoming to be "imminent." The agency found itself in the precarious position of keeping this particular family apart for the good of the children who wanted to be home with their parents despite the exceptional quality of life they enjoyed as the agency's wards. In Dorchester's Bradshaw House, where we lived after Brighton, the pattern continued. We told our caseworker that we were happy there, for it was like summer camp. "They go swimming, have activities and play games," he agreed. "However, they expect to go back home in the Fall."

The agency warily maintained consistent and emotionally supportive contact with our parents and monitored our mother's physical and psychological status through communication with hospital doctors and social workers, all in the interest of rehabilitating the Gordon family as soon as that might become possible. In fact, because the agency seriously entertained the possibility of our returning soon to our parents, it arranged for us to attend schools near our Roxbury address. We began the academic year by taking advantage of that proximity, flouting agency policy and, for the few weeks our stratagem remained undetected by the agency, visiting our mother at home almost every day after school.

One over-riding fact remained constant as long as our mother lived: regardless of the anxiety and uncertainty characteristic of life at home, and despite the exceptional quality of our lives in the agency's group homes, Mike and I wanted to return home as intensely as our mother wanted us to be there. I believe this to be true but must admit that the issue was loaded with doubt and apprehension on everyone's part.

Regardless of the issue's complexity, any plans to effect our return to our parents were abandoned when, on September 26, 1952, the hospital communicated to the agency its opinion that our mother's apparent recovery was "symptomatic," that "it would disappear," that her prognosis was "guarded," and that it was her doctors' opinion that she was "not ready" to resume her maternal responsibilities. It fell to Edward Portnoy, newly appointed caseworker for all the boys at Bradshaw House, to tell Mike and me why we would not be going home "just yet." I responded to Portnoy's news by telling him that we already knew this, and that maybe we would be able to go home "after the winter."

In the year of life remaining to our mother after receiving the doctors' judgment she would continue to voice her wish that Mike and I live at home once she had recovered from her illness. But she spoke to Portnoy of her reluctance to have us return home because of the likelihood that we would live in fear of another relapse of her insanity. It was Portnoy's impression, however, that it was she who lived in fear "that she might disappoint [us] again."

My heart aches for this woman who desperately wanted to be a good mother, to live with us and to care for us. Regardless of her efforts to do so she knew it was never to be.

MIKE AND I WOULD LEARN TO LIVE
IN OUR NEW COMMUNITY

IT WASN'T ALWAYS EASY

"Home"

We were big kids now. We were going to live in Bradshaw House, in Dorchester. We were going to leave the home in Brighton, where the little boys and girls lived, where we had lived until now, and live with big boys who had had their bar mitzvahs. Mike had not, but he was to go with me and we would be together, as our parents wanted us to be from the start. That's what Mr. Portnoy told us that morning, calling us over to him after breakfast as the other kids left the dining room, asking us to sit and surprising us with the news.

We had learned a lot in Brighton. We had learned at every meal to stand behind our chair before eating and to put one hand on our head (instead of a yamulka) and say in Hebrew the *borucha* for bread, thanking God. We had learned how to help Mike Fay in his workshop downstairs, to listen carefully to his instructions, pleased that we were able to care for the bunny. We had learned to walk on different streets to a different grammar school and the names of different teachers and different students. We had learned about Esther and Mordecai and Haman and the holiday of Purim and about Chanukah and about how to build a succah on Succoth and its delicious piney smell. We had learned to get along without our mother and father, to see our father on some weekends, and our mother almost never, for she was in the hospital or at home, as then, on Seaver Street, too sick to see us, our father said.

We had learned all of this and much more in Brighton, and to learn these things we needed time, and so the white house with the broad front steps and the tall pillars and the magnolia tree that dropped its pink petals onto the lawn seemed almost like home to us. So when Mr. Portnoy told Mike and me as we sat in the sunlight slanting through the window blinds in the empty dining room that we would soon be going to Dorchester to live we almost didn't believe him.

Mr. Portnoy was my social worker and I liked him. I liked the way he winked at me, and how he spoke, softly, as if unwilling to frighten me. After my eye operation he brought me chocolate bonbons in a green box, but I never told him I could not eat them because they made me sick. (Everything made me sick except ginger ale). I didn't want to hurt his feelings.

So I trusted him even when the things he wanted me to do made me unhappy, as when he told me he wanted me to talk with a doctor. I said no, I didn't need to see a doctor, there was nothing wrong with me. But Mr. Portnoy told me just to try it, Benjy, just try it. And so I went with him to see the doctor in a big building and we went up in an elevator and walked down a hall and opened a cloudy glass door and went in and I sat down in a leather chair and the doctor came in and sat on the other side of the desk and Mr. Portnoy said he would be just in the waiting room and he left me there.

The doctor said his name was Doctor Platt and he said he was going to show me some pictures, and I was supposed to tell him what they made me think. I said o.k. and he showed me the pictures slowly and one at a time. They were ink pictures, as if someone had spilled ink on white paper and folded the paper and unfolded it and let it dry. I remember only one of them. It was all bright red and looked as if it had wings and it made me think of a flying cardinal and I told Doctor Platt that and I told him what I thought about the other pictures and he wrote things down on a yellow pad of paper and then he said that wasn't so bad was it? and I said no and he asked me to come again one more time and I said I would. Mr. Portnoy took me home after we had ice cream in heavy silver dishes in Brighams and we made plans to come back one more time.

The next time the doctor had a notebook and he kept looking at something in it and looking at me and looking at it again and then he looked at me and told me I was afraid. I felt my head get tight and I said I wasn't afraid and what did he mean and what was I afraid of. And he said I was afraid that my mother was going to die and that I was afraid to think about it or talk about it or it might come true. And I began to cry even though I didn't want him to see me cry but I cried anyway and I couldn't stop. Mr. Portnoy came and we went back to Brighton and we didn't stop for ice cream.

But this time I wasn't unhappy, even though I was going to leave Brighton, because we were big kids and we were going to be with other big kids in Dorchester. Mr. Portnoy told us on the ride there that we would miss some things about Brighton but that we would soon forget them and get to know new things. He said Mrs. Roshelitz's blintzes were a miracle and he turned his head and winked at me. During our ride I peered through the car's windows at our surroundings and that evening I told Mike my idea.

The next morning, right after breakfast, we were on our way. We had never been on Bradshaw Street, but its trees and crowded houses and little lawns right up to the sidewalk made it feel like one of the streets we did know near Blue Hill Ave. We knew on which corner of Blue Hill Ave. and one of those streets we could sit at the soda fountain and drink root beer in big frosty glass mugs. We knew on which corner to find the Franklin Park Theater: a quarter allowed each of us two feature films, an episode of Flash Gordon, a Popeye cartoon and the newsreel. We knew where the streetcar stopped, the one that took us to the Chez Vous to go roller skating on the big oval rink or play with the pinball machines if we had any dimes. And we knew how to take that streetcar to the Oriental Theater in Mattapan, where alien creatures with bright green eyes squatted in alcoves and just by looking up at the ceiling you could see hundreds of stars. We knew all of this because Blue Hill Ave. was almost our old neighborhood, running with the streetcar tracks along one side of Franklin Park, then diverging from the tracks as they ran along another side of the park and Seaver Street to home.

We were on our way to Seaver Street to see our mother and father, to surprise them and be together with them, maybe even for the whole day until it was time to go back. But we wouldn't take the streetcar because we had no money. Sometimes we would take the streetcar because we could go to the back and turn the big curved handle and stomp down hard again and again on the metal pedal to make the clanking sound to warn people on the track. The real conductors didn't mind and all the kids did it when they got the chance. But this time Mike and I would walk.

We crossed Blue Hill Ave. when the traffic light turned red, looking both ways anyway, and we went into the park and followed some paths and left the paths to walk over the hilly part where kids who lived in Dorchester near the park sledded in the winter. Mike and I had a Speedway sled with red runners but we sledded in the park closer to our apartment building, in Roxbury. We walked over the hills but it was early in the morning and we didn't see any kids.

And we didn't see any kids when we got near the birdcage where big birds lived in a giant dome next to the birdhouse. We and our friends would sit on the flat, sloping metal caps of the fence around the birdcage and watch the blue peacocks and the other birds and sometimes in summer there would be elephants in there, too, walking slowly and dragging their trunks along the ground and throwing straw and dirt onto their backs. The birds knew how to stay away from the elephants and seemed not to mind sharing the cage with them. We would sit there watching the peacocks and the toucans and the elephants and eating candy from the boxes we bought at the round candy stand made of branches that looked like a house in Africa might look but without the Cracker Jacks and the Necco Wafers and little boxes of animal crackers on the counter behind wire grilles. We would sit there and feel the warmth of the metal fence under the sun and listen to the shrill cries of the peacocks and smell the funky smell of the elephants and slowly eat our Cracker Jacks.

But we didn't stop at the birdcage. We walked through the rose garden where all the paths had even borders and went at right angles to each other and the rose stems climbed wooden trellises or stood in neat beds. But there were no roses because it was still spring and the grass was pale and last year's leaves on the rose bushes were brown and curled up and brittle to the touch. Mama loved the rose garden. She and I and Mike would go there and sit on a wooden bench and just be quiet because it was so pretty, she said, and deserved to be appreciated in silence. Sometimes we would just walk on the paths and then we would go to the candy stand and we would each get a Hoodsie and eat it slowly on the way home with the flat wooden spoons.

From there Mike and I could see the row of apartment buildings on Seaver Street and we walked out of the park near the shed where people waited for the streetcar to Mattapan or Egleston Square. Sometimes Mike and I would wait there with our mother for our father to come home from work if he finished work in the afternoon and once when I was very little and playing there in the dirt with my red shovel I swung it at a bee and the bee stung me and when I cried Mama picked me up and hugged me and I could smell her perfume, like roses, and she told me not to cry, that it wasn't so bad and that the bee hurt more because it had died and I felt bad about that and stopped crying. There was no one in the shed and we crossed the tracks and waited for a chance to cross

47

Seaver Street properly and did because when we and our friends were little our mothers wouldn't let us cross the street to go into the park until we knew how to do it properly. And then we were there, standing in front of the door to our apartment building, and we went in.

We wanted it to be a surprise so we didn't press the little black button near our name and our mailbox but pushed open the heavy inside door and entered the hall and heard the door close behind us with a whoosh and walked past Mrs. Sandler's and Mrs. Goldberg's apartment doors and the stairs to go up and the door to the big courtyard and into the little ante-room where the door on the left went to our apartment, across from the cellar. The light bulb was on, hanging above us, and we stood there for a moment and we smiled at each other and then, together, we knocked.

It was quiet. I could hear Mike breathing and my own breath. We stood still. I thought I could hear a truck pass on Seaver Street, but inside there was no sound. We stood and listened, each of us leaning slightly toward the door. And then I heard something happen. It was my father getting up from the chair with the white doilies on its arms. We heard his two steps toward the door and then it opened. My father stood there, looking down at us. He was wearing a white undershirt and you could see hairs on his chest near the edges. His face was dark with whiskers. He looked at us and said nothing and then he said "What are you doing here?"

Mike and I stood in the dim light of the bulb and I told him that we were now staying in Bradshaw House in Dorchester and that we had walked from there that morning to surprise him and Mama. He said no one had told him that we had been moved and then my mother was in the doorway asking "Who is it, Josh?" and then she saw us and she was quiet but her face looked happy to see us and my father told her what I had told him and she told us to come in and my father said to come in and we did.

Our mother went into her bedroom to put on something nicer, she said. Our father went into the kitchen and we followed him and he got a glass of water from the sink and he smiled at us and asked us if we wanted some water and we said yes we did and we sat at the table and he brought us glasses filled with water and sat down too and we all waited. The plates with the French soldiers and the French words were still on the wall and I tried to read the words as I always did and then I looked out the window and saw the little courtyard where we played ball against the wall and the driveway and the empty lot and then my mother came.

She went to the refrigerator in the corner with the silver wings on the door and the silver handle and opened the door and stood there looking in and said there was no food but only milk and a Hershey bar and it was sunday and too early for the grocery store to be open anyway and she was sorry. She stood there by the refrigerator with the door open and turned to us and said we should have a glass of milk, that we must be thirsty after our walk, and then we could share the candy bar. Our father told her to shut the door and to sit down with us so we could talk and she did.

Our father asked us about Bradshaw House and we told him about the boys there but we didn't know their names yet and we told him about Frank and that he was nice and about our room with the bunk beds and about the oatmeal and raisins and brown sugar that morning. And he asked how we had left after breakfast and we told him we just left.

Our mother said they must be worried about us. Her face looked very sad and the white parts of her eyes had lots of red lines in them and I thought she must have been crying but I didn't say anything about that. I said we hadn't thought about that but couldn't we call them and our father said that was a good idea and he got up and went into the living room and soon I heard him take the receiver from the phone on the table and dialing and I heard him talking and then he put the receiver back and came back to the kitchen. He stood near the table and looked at us and I saw the gray folds of flesh beneath his eyes and he smiled at us and he said we would have to go back to Bradshaw House because Mama needed to rest.

I wanted to tell him that Mike and I could help take care of Mama when he went to work or even when he was home but I didn't say anything about that either. Our mother didn't say anything but she kept nodding as if she were having a conversation and then she said we should have the milk and Hershey bar before we left. She stood and turned to the refrigerator and pulled the door open again and took out the bottle of milk and the brown package of chocolate and went to the shelf over the sink and took down our favorite glasses, the ones with Popeye and the Lone Ranger on them, and poured the milk and gave us the full glasses and peeled the paper and the silver foil from the squares of chocolate and laid them down on the table and sat down again and watched us while we ate.

When we left with our father she was standing in the doorway, waving, but when I looked back again I couldn't see her anymore. We went across Seaver Street and stood in the shed and waited for the streetcar. Inside it said "Kilroy was here" in big black letters. In a little while the streetcar came. It was orange and squealed on the rails when it stopped. It was almost empty and we sat with our father on the long wooden bench, Mike on one side and I on the other. When we got off I remembered that Mike and I had not thought to play the conductor game.

On the way to Bradshaw House we had to walk fast because our father was tall and he took big steps. When we got there we could see the boys playing in the back yard, throwing darts at a target painted on a big board. Our father told us to play with the boys and we watched them while he went inside to talk to Frank.

When he came out he came over to us and said hello to the other boys and took us to the sidewalk and told us he was sorry we couldn't stay longer at home because Mama needed to rest but maybe soon she would be better and we could come then. He bent to kiss us goodbye and when it was my turn I moved my head a little bit away and my father looked at me and he had large brown eyes and he asked me if I was ashamed to have the boys see him kissing me and I said no, that wasn't why, and he looked at me and he kissed me again but he didn't hug me.

I watched my father walk alone up the street toward Blue Hill Ave. and then I went over to the boys playing darts and watched for a while and then I went back to the sidewalk and I couldn't see my father and then I ran and ran and ran to catch up to him, looking down at the sidewalk and seeing the parallel lines rush past and I was panting and sweaty when I got to Blue Hill Ave. and my father was standing on the median and the streetcar hadn't come yet and I ran across the street to him without even looking for cars and hugged him and he looked at me and he hugged me and he said I had better be going back and then the streetcar came and my father got on and he waved to me and I waved to him and then I walked home.

Best Standards

Mike and I and the other children in the Brighton study home were largely unaware of being "studied" by our houseparents and caseworkers. Nor did we concern ourselves with awareness that we were being prepared by the agency to live with foster families if our natural parents should prove unable to care for us. That level of understanding could wait until we were old enough to live in Bradshaw House, when the prospect of foster home placement would become a reality. Yes, we met with our caseworkers every other week in interviews meant to assess our opinions of life in the home as well as our general wellbeing. But our chief concerns were the daily realities of home and school. These moved us toward the regularity and sense of normality we required. That process began for Mike and me as soon as we awoke to the first morning of our lives in Brighton.

Mike was already awake and talking when I swam to consciousness that morning. I kept my eyes shut and listened as he explained to two boys our appearance in the small bedroom. When I chose to open my eyes there was no need to discuss that further and soon we were in the bathroom brushing our teeth and washing our faces and hands before rushing with several boys and girls down the broad stairway to the dining room where breakfast awaited us.

Taking our cues from the other children, Mike and I stood behind our chairs and put our hands on our heads. We knew nothing of the words they spoke although we understood they were prayers for the food we were to eat, prayers we would learn almost immediately and recite before every meal we ate at the long tables in that room. After we sat the man who had taken us in the evening before welcomed Mike and me, told the children our names and reminded everyone that it was a school day and that there would be time later to get to know each other. We watched intently as the boys and girls took their brown bag lunches from a counter in the kitchen, ran to the broad front stairs, and headed up the nearby street to school. Soon Mike and I walked with the man up that street to the Winship school. By the end of the school day we were "registered," assigned to home rooms and classes, and ready the next day with the other children to pick up from the big counter our own brown bag lunches. Although we had walked hundreds of times to and from our previous school, the Garrison, in Roxbury, it now seemed as distant from our present reality as our mother and father.

While dinner was the featured attraction every evening, there were after-school snacks and "activities" to keep us busy and organized, as well as time to play before doing our homework.

"Activity persons" came regularly to instruct us in arts and crafts and in singing and dancing. Jeannette Alpert taught me to paint and glaze upon a white plate the sumptuously attired Mordecai and his bejeweled horse. It leaned gaily against the wall on its shelf over the kitchen sink in our drab Roxbury apartment long after my mother had died. Red-faced Mike Fay, the handyman, was always ready to bring us into his projects, as when we built with brick and mortar the outdoor fireplace. In preparation for my bar mitzvah, Rabbi Joseph Shubow of Temple B'nai Moshe came to instruct me in Hebrew in the little room filled with light beneath the eaves.

Today, Leonard Serkess remembers his leadership in establishing the policies which allowed children to move from the insecurities of family dysfunction toward emotional strength. He talks with great authority and gusto of the role he played in applying progressive principles to the difficult circumstances in which we needy Jewish children found ourselves. Even before he became the home's director he argued that its large-group organization, a vestige of the former regime, did not lend itself to the children's preparation for family life and urged that it be modified "to create a feeling of home life" and a "family atmosphere . . . where the child could test himself further for his ability to go into a foster home or his own home." That family atmosphere increasingly became the norm during my and Mike's residence in Brighton, Newton, Dorchester and Winthrop.

Serkess made a point of demonstrating to us that, while our own family circumstances were unfortunate, we were not to think of ourselves as objects of charity. There would be, for instance, no more donations of used clothes, no more pushkies, and no more free-for-alls for pennies.

The agency often employed Pauline Fox to take us, individually, into Boston to acquire new clothes. At other times it was our caseworker who took us. I remember Mrs. Fox as a stylishly dressed woman who spoke warmly to me of her family and of vacationing at Nantasket Beach, south of Boston. It must have been difficult for both parties—Pauline and her charge—to walk the tightrope between sure knowledge that we were children who relied upon charity and the attempt to foster an understanding in us that we were worthy individuals despite that reliance. We all knew that the process of selecting clothes from gray boxes in department store stock rooms carried with it an amorphous stigma; but the clothes, themselves, managed to contradict that stigma's substance. They affirmed our personal value.

And then there was the exception in my case which proved the rule: the bright red woolen v-neck sweater I coveted, knowing it was not to be for me, not included on the list of clothes I was to obtain on that shopping expedition. Mrs. Fox saw what must have been apparent to any observant onlooker and bought it for me. While I do not remember wearing it afterward, I know I must have done so with great pleasure, set apart as I was from all others.

Several photographs reveal the pride we boys and girls in Brighton felt in ourselves, dressed for festive occasions in our own new and stylish clothes. I think of one in particular: My brother and I are intensely aware of the camera; my right arm is about his shoulders; he stands rigidly, but playfully, at attention; I am smiling broadly: the two of us are obviously delighted with our bran new three-button suits and our spit-polished shoes. More meaningfully, we seem happy about ourselves.

Then there were the "pushkies", the cans and boxes that for many years stood on the counters of local merchants, soliciting customers to contribute to the welfare of the children in the home just up the street from Brighton Center. It was not unusual for the children to see these, as the stores were within easy walking distance, and their sense of personal worth must have been consistently challenged by their being so blatantly defined as objects of charity, even as they laughingly deposited their own pennies into the pushky's slot.

Soon the pushkies disappeared from the counters, as defunct as the long-standing practice by the ladies of the Helping Hand Auxiliary, the home's prior administration, of throwing pennies onto the home's parquet floor in order that the children might enjoy the healthy diversion of scrambling after them. (Many years later I watched with dismay from the deck of a ship in the harbor of Corfu as wealthy tourists amused themselves by throwing coins into the water so that poor children might dive for them).

In the perennial interest of the children's self-esteem, Serkess even discontinued the ordering of canned institutional-grade vegetables destined for the home's kitchen, not because of any inferiority in quality, but because their sometimes oddly proportioned pieces fostered a belief that the children were required to eat leftovers.

These and other policies defined a context in which Mike and I and the other children in the study home could grow stronger. From 1946, when it assumed control of the home, the agency was determined to create in Brighton a temporary but stable and supportive environment, a nurturing family life that we could not take for granted in our own families, with our own parents.

This was also the norm for the adolescents in Bradshaw House. A tall, robust woman, Mrs. Roshelitz cooked for the boys there. She had been a refugee from Europe's Holocaust and brought to America a rich knowledge of Judaic ethnic dishes. (Years later I would recognize her spirit in the women who cooked and served meals in the Atran Center for Jewish Culture's kitchen just off Madison Avenue in Manhattan. Within the context of Ethnic Studies field trips I brought my students from their suburban high school and encouraged them to try the strange dishes—the borscht with sour cream, the crispy potato latkes, the pruney tsimmis—served by welcoming women with numbers on their forearms. When I went there alone to eat the women asked, like grandmothers, "Mr. Gordon, where are the darlinks?").

How many times did I peer into the kitchen from the shadow of the doorway to see Mrs. Roshelitz at the great black stove and ask, "Mrs. Roshelitz, will you make blintzes today?" For her blintzes were not of this world and never to be equaled in my lifetime. They were long, perhaps eight or nine inches long, fat and sweet and topped by mounds of sour cream. And not only did they contain the rich farmer's cheese, but dark raisins! We could never have enough. It seems to me in retrospect that Mrs. Roshelitz offered her wonderful blintzes to us boys with the love that a mother feels for her children and with the painful knowledge of their vulnerability to the world's hazards. I was unable to articulate this impression at the time, but somehow I knew it to be so.

Photographs of children enjoying a Thanksgiving dinner and a Passover seder around well-appointed tables in the Brighton home suggest the significant role played by personal clothing and carefully prepared food in creating a family whose members appear to be comfortable and even happy.

Whether carving the turkey or standing proudly with formally dressed boys and girls in anticipation of a family-style meal, Serkess strove to be an exemplary role model whose comportment reinforced his determination that his extended family members should feel worthy and right about themselves. He remembers pressuring a housemother to resign because she continued to wear clothes he deemed inappropriate in a salutary family context. And he delights in recalling how he and his bride-to-be invited all twenty-two of the children then living in the home to their wedding. (The Serkesses lived in the home for three years before moving to nearby accommodations; they knew they had reached the limits of constructing an extended family when they discovered giggling adolescent girls beneath their bed)!

The Passover seders; the shabbat meals every Friday evening; the painting and singing introductions to Jewish history and culture; the rabbinical instruction in preparation for bar mitzvah ceremonies; and regular celebrations of Jewish holidays such as Succoth and Chanukah all reinforced our understanding that we belonged to the still greater extended family of Judaism. To that end the agency gave me a scarlet velveteen bag upon which was boldly sewn in gold a large Jewish star. In the bag were my new tallis and white silken yarmulke, as well as the leather tifillin whose strangeness and purpose I never did understand. Walking to and from the synagogue, I carried this bag with a self-conscious pride in my Jewishness and with a knowledge of my cultural roots that contributed to my emotional strength. My copy of *The Holy Scriptures*, presented to me by Brotherhood B'nai Moshe upon the occasion of my bar mitzvah, reminded me of my Jewish family ties and responsibilities.

Having said this, I must pause, first with a smile at how casually enforced was the inculcation of Jewish culture, then with some discomfort as I recall a painful consequence of that casualness. These trips to and from the synagogue, for instance, were sporadic, never insisted upon or even encouraged by Serkess or his staff, many of whom were not Jewish and all of whom must have been challenged by the process of readying and transporting children to Saturday morning prayers. Even when I walked alone to the synagogue I did so without great enthusiasm, as I disliked sitting through the lengthy religious services conducted in a language I did not understand.

And besides, the dominant secular culture was impossible to escape even if one wanted to, which I did not. Had I not been chosen by my teachers at the Winship School to play a significant part in the school's Christmas pageant? I certainly was pleased. There must have been some knowing smiles in the audience when I stood upon the tinseled stage to declaim the lines that recalled part of the Christmas story: "I is for the innkeeper, who had no room to give . . ." Even within the home's holiday celebration I was delightedly cast by my housefather in the role of an angel, grandly winged with wire and toilet paper and wearing only my white underpants as I descended the ornate staircase framed by pink and green stained glass window panels. I was to be of service to the magi.

I believe we flourished in the relatively unregimented group environments in which we lived as agency wards. That unauthorized trek with Mike through Franklin Park to see our parents, for instance, was at the time a wonderful adventure as far as we were concerned. Despite its disappointing outcome, it satisfied for the moment a pressing need to be with our parents, however briefly. But within the casual supervisory framework that made that satisfaction possible, important things sometimes slipped through the cracks, as the following anecdote demonstrates.

It is November, gray and chill. We are gathered by my mother's tombstone. My father is there. Standing by his side, I look up at him. His face is drawn. There are gray pouches beneath his eyes. The rabbi is there, and my brother, and my aunts and uncles. I had been told earlier that week of the planned unveiling ceremony, when a cloth would be removed from my mother's new tombstone and when prayers would be said to remember her and to honor God. So now I am content to listen to the rabbi as he speaks about my mother and prays by her grave. And then he looks at me and Mike and my father and asks that we lead the family in saying Kaddish.

It is as if he had hit me in the face with the back of his hand. Kaddish? I do not know the prayer. The rabbi, who had spent hours teaching me Hebrew in preparation for my bar mitzvah, had never taught me it. He had never thought to do so. No one had. I am humiliated as I stand there and listen to my father chant the rhythmic and sonorous passages and to conceal my shame I mumble gibberish. No one will ever mention this disgrace to me, not my father, not the rabbi, but the depth of my embarrassment lingers even until the moment I write of it.

And although I can still taste the cream cheese and sweet cherries I bought and ate while on a solitary expedition to Grove Hall, happily spitting the smooth pits into the gutter—that is to say, while I can still taste the delicious freedom of the moment—my adult perspective compels me to acknowledge the potentially hazardous consequences of such freedom.

Besides, words used above—words like "flourished" and "wonderful" and "delicious" as well as those sunny references to our clothes' and meals' making it possible to "feel right about ourselves"—are beginning to ring false, or at least not completely true. That is not to deny the truth of our extraordinarily good fortune to be under the agency's supervision; but that good fortune in no way insured our happiness. A happy child does not single out to abuse and torment with shrieks and venom another child who is clearly miserable, frequently in tears, always needing the presence of a sympathetic houseparent, as I did Norman. A happy child does not run in tears from the festively adorned room where Chanukah presents are being distributed, crying hysterically that his brother had received a shiny, red football helmet and he . . . not. (Today I cannot recall the gift I received, but whatever it was didn't make me "feel right" about myself). A happy child does not run to the bathroom and lock himself in when he encounters real or perceived threats, as both Mike and I were wont to do. No, we were not happy—why should we be?—and we did our best to conceal our unhappiness and its source from ourselves as well as from all others. The suggestion that we were happy only continues a fundamentally dishonest pattern that can do no good for anyone.

"Communication"

When Mike and I were little and our mother was sick, I went with Aunt Marion and Uncle Leo and Mike went with Aunt Natalie and Uncle Hiram and we were both gone from Seaver Street for a long time. In Haverhill, I thought about our games of stickball and punchball in the empty lot next to our apartment building and about playing King, Queen, Jack, Out with a pinky ball against the wall next to Mrs. Sandler's window. I remembered how we played until we could hardly see through the gathering night and how only then did my friends and I end our game and heed our mothers' calls to come in for supper. I remembered how my mother and Mrs. Cohen hung white sheets from window clotheslines and pasted paper black cats and orange pumpkins on them and filled a big pot with water and floated apples with nickels and dimes in them in the water and how all the neighborhood came and stayed until dark.

In Haverhill I sat quietly at the dinner table with my aunt and uncle and was careful to chew my food with my mouth closed and slept in the little room upstairs where my cousin Eugene slept before he moved away and had a house of his own, my aunt said. Often I was on my knees in the back yard watching the little dirt mounds where the ants lived and the ants carrying things or fighting or moving without any purpose that I could tell, or in the front, throwing my ball against the steps and catching it or running after it and imagining that my friends would come and play with me and that Ted Williams was riding by and he would see me and stop his car and come to me and ask me to join the Red Sox.

When Mike and I came home and hugged our mother as she bent down for a kiss I knew that things would never be the same. It was the way it felt when she hugged me, as if she were a thin pane of glass. When she stood up she held her chin higher than she used to, as if posing for a photograph, and smiled more widely than she used to and everything inside my head felt tight.

She made meatloaf that evening, my favorite, the kind with the eggs in it and the vegetables all around the edges and apologized for it, saying it wasn't very good, and talked about the burnt place on the table where Uncle Shuval had forgotten his cigarette. My father told us to make sure to eat our bread and my mother went to bed early and didn't speak at all of what had happened to her and to me and Mike in the time she and we had been away.

Afterwards, lying in our beds in the darkness, Mike and I didn't talk about being away from our home or our parents or our friends or each other. It was as if nothing had happened. I felt limp and empty, as a kicked ball might feel if it could feel. At school my friends asked where we had been and they asked why we had been there and I would not talk about it to them or to anyone, not even to Mrs. Brown, but Mrs. Brown never asked me, only looked at me sadly from behind her desk. Sometimes, if I went alone, I cried soundlessly on my way home from school, walking on the dirt path behind the anonymous apartment buildings, thinking about my mother and the things we used to do together, like hanging up the laundry. I would grunt as I lifted the heavy basket of wet clothes and carry it from the apartment to the big courtyard and my mother would tell me how strong I was and sometimes the clothesline was low enough for me to reach and then she would give me the wooden clothespins so I could hang things up.

But things were not like that now. It was as if my mother were floating away and I could not catch up to her and keep her from leaving and as if a mother who was not my real mother lived with my father and Mike and me and we couldn't talk to her and she couldn't talk to us and soon she was in the hospital again and she was not to be visited, my father said, even by me and Mike and we lived in the Bradshaw House with Danny and Gerry and the other boys and Frank.

So when Frank said our father was coming to tell us something important and that we were to spend the day with him the moment seemed to me as familiar and inevitable as each part of the frequent dream from which I would wake with terrified cries and rush to my parents' bed for assurance that it had been just a dream, that everything would be alright.

It was just a dream, Benjy, my mother would say.

Don't be afraid, Benjy, my father would say. Go back to bed.

And I would climb into my mother's and father's bed and wedge myself between them and feel the warmth of their bodies and try to forget the facts and the feelings of what had been just a dream.

Waiting on the sidewalk for my father to come, I remembered the way my apartment always appeared in my dream. Vague the standing radio in a corner of the living room, blurry the scrolled back of the rocking chair in my bedroom, draped in fog the dishes on the kitchen shelves, all as my mother, herself, appeared, as if she were marooned within her own translucence as she gave me the prescription for the medicine to ask of the man in the white jacket in the drugstore. I had made the actual trip to the drugstore many times and the man always knew what I wanted before I asked for it but I always carried the doctor's prescription anyway, just in case, as my mother said. But in the dream there was no room for contingency and I had no choice but to observe each of its inevitable segments, as if my anxiety were spreading like an incoming tide and establishing dominion over everything I futilely endeavored to understand within and beyond my home.

I would shut behind me the wooden door to the apartment and hold my breath while rushing by the menacing cellar. I would slow my pace in the narrow hallway at the end of which, through the two glass doors, I could see the sunlit street. Everything would be familiar: Mrs. Sandler's and Mrs. Goldberg's apartment doors, the mass of the hallway door as I pulled it open, the two marble steps downward into the foyer where the mailboxes were set into one wall, the wall itself against which Mike and I and Stan and Steve tossed our waxed baseball cards, and finally the door to the street, 132 in gilt on its top windowpane. Familiar, but somehow compromised, obscure, somehow wrong.

And it was wrong as I walked by the empty lot where we played ball and built our tree house, wrong all the way down Humboldt Avenue to the drugstore, wrong as I silently received the little bag from the smiling man in white, wrong on my return, as if I were walking in an impenetrable mist. And then I heard the great muffled bells, frightening because so unfamiliar, for there were no bells in my little part of Roxbury.

And now I was running headlong to my mother, to home, pushing past the heavy doors, even forgetting to hold my breath by the cellar. I stood, beating my fists upon the swirling grain of the apartment door crying Mama Mama and the door opened and an impossibly old woman stood there scowling at me and I cried You're not my mother You're not my mother again and again and woke up crying and I knew without question and despite anything my parents might say that this had not been just a dream, that it had been something more than a dream, that it concerned loss past and loss to come, and that I had every reason to be afraid.

And, waiting, I remembered my mother as I had last seen her, almost transparent in her white nightgown as she propped herself up against the mahogany hope chest in the living room. Determined to cook supper for Mike and me, who were visiting for the day, she moved torturously toward the kitchen while she intoned what I would later come to know as the twenty-third psalm.

Waiting, I knew I should be able to act like a man and deny my childish tears and the bitter and unspoken knowledge they represented. Had not the rabbi said I was a man? Just after I read my section from the Torah and chanted the final prayers of my bar mitzvah ceremony, had he not pounced upon me like a brawny, black-bearded cat and gripped my arm beneath the tallis I wore for the occasion, the silky white prayer shawl with pretty blue stripes, and spoken to the small congregation of the difficult life I had lived in so short a time? And without hope of escape until granted it, had I not looked down at the narrow boards of the stage and felt my cheeks grow warm as I listened to the rabbi speak of my new status as a man within the Jewish faith? But my eyes were heavy with wet and I feared I would be unable to prevent its sliding down my cheeks and onto the sidewalk where I waited with my brother that late November morning for my father to come.

And then he came, a tall man with large brown, sad eyes, wearing a gray tweed overcoat and a gray fedora and he stood with Mike and me in front of the homely building in which we lived and he knelt down and put his large hands on our shoulders and said to us God took Mama away and soon we were in Uncle Hiram's car driving to Wellesley where Aunt Minnette lived with Aunt Dina and I played pick-up-sticks with my cousins Jackie and Ken and had hamburgers with mustard and relish that Uncle Jim cooked on the grill and filled my mouth and chewed and laughed and I saw the confusion in my cousin Arnie's glance but ignored it and played pick-up-sticks some more.

It was dark when Mike and I returned to Bradshaw House and stood again with our father on the same sidewalk and I looked up to kiss my father who bent down to receive the kiss and give me one of his own and hugged us and said goodnight and said everything would be alright, and got into the passenger seat of Uncle Hiram's car and waved goodbye and rode away and the day was almost over.

Inside everything was quiet and still. It was dark climbing the familiar stairs, turning left at the top and walking down the hall and into our room where other boys slept in their bunks, sighing, as if sharing in whispers their secret lives.

In the darkness Mike and I undressed and got into our beds and I knew that my brother was still awake long after we had done so, lying like me on his back and looking up at the darkness in the room. And I knew too that it would be Mike who broke the silence that lay between us as if it were an appendage of the darkness, heavy and without definition.

"Poor Mama," Mike said.

"Shut up," I said.

And that was all we ever said about it.

HERSZL SINGER'S GIFT OF GORKY
TO MIKE AND BURTON?

Emotional Poverty

It has been fascinating and, to say the least, not a little unsettling to learn from the case files what others thought of Mike and me. Upon our second placement in the study home our caseworker, Sylvia Chayet, remarked that we appeared "to be in need of a great deal of help in the physical and emotional areas." But our refusal to discuss our negative emotions then or afterward, or even to admit that we had any, made casework on our behalf a consistent challenge.

Twice in our first year as agency wards we were referred to a clinical psychologist, Dr. Henry Platt, to determine, among other things, to what extent our family history had influenced our "present and possible future functioning," to gain an appreciation of our "capacities and limitations," and to learn to what extent, if any, "emotional blocking" was affecting our progress. Platt evaluated us a third time, two years later, after our mother died. He intended his assessments to serve as aids to the agency's further planning for us. They indicate the depth of our need for emotional support and our adamant refusal to accommodate those who sought to help us acknowledge that need rather than repress it. Platt and our caseworkers articulated this consistent dynamic over a five-year period.

Mike, for instance, "contributed very little" to one of his early interviews with Platt, who found it impossible to draw him into any conversation about our mother. In fact, he seemed to show no concern regarding our mother's illness, assumed it was quite temporary, and looked forward to going home soon to our parents. Platt concluded:

> Emotional deprivation is reflected. Michael seeks love and affection but is reluctant to become too emotionally involved with others in order to receive this. He is a very shaky lad, who has probably experienced many disappointments in life and he tends to look upon others with an air of suspicion. He is fearful of changes and new situations, tending to become panicky at prospects of becoming involved in unfamiliar situations. There is a free floating anxiety and he acknowledges on testing that he is "worried about different things."

In Platt's professional judgment, Mike was "an emotionally cold, rigid, insecure, anxious youngster" who "maintained a system of very tight ego defenses" that led him "to shy away from affective stimulation." As tensions increase, Platt wrote, Mike's "rigid defenses crumble and he acts out with impulsive, aggressive behavior." Surprisingly, considering this bleak evaluation of Mike's personality, Platt had no particular recommendations to offer and predicted that Mike would continue to make a satisfactory adjustment to the study home and to school "with proper sympathetic understanding."

Platt intended these clinical judgments to refer only to Mike although they certainly characterized some of my psychological makeup at that time as well as after our mother's death. Early in my stay in the study home he administered to me a battery of tests whose results revealed that while "on the surface there seems to be little concern over the mother figure, projected testing suggests considerable anxiety over a non-nurturant mother image." This anxiety seems to have been graphically revealed in a figure drawing I made of an "obvious" mother image: "Her hands," Platt wrote, "are drawn short and so close to the body that they serve to suggest some breast displacement. She is not giving of herself or receiving from the outside."

My pose of equanimity in the face of my family's trials did not convince Platt any more than did my denial of anxiety regarding my relationship with my mother. While I seemed "on the surface" to be better adjusted than Michael, he suggested, "much of this may be on a superficial basis." As tensions rise "Benjamin finds it difficult to maintain his facade of well-being and appears to act out his anxiety with explosive behavior." Although Platt does not specifically mention it in his report, I remember crying hard in his office when he shared some of his conclusions with me.

Testing after my mother's death, Platt reported, revealed that I was "emotionally maladjusted" and exhibited "strong depressive tendencies." During the "interview situation" I had "maintained a rather rigid and expressionless façade, constantly on guard to prevent being brought into discussing emotionally charged materials." Since I had no problems, I told the good doctor, I saw "little point" in discussing problems with him or with anyone else at the agency.

"It would appear," Platt opined, that I was functioning well and that "emotional factors are not interfering with such functioning." As in Mike's case, and just as surprising to me today, he had little in the line of recommendations to suggest, only that I be provided "with sufficient opportunity to develop [my] very fine creative tendencies." Only once, in concluding his evaluation of my emotional status after my mother's death, did Platt suggest that my symptoms might warrant further psychiatric treatment. He wrote: "Psychiatric consultation is suggested." But there is no hint in the case files that this modest suggestion, whatever it meant, was ever discussed or pursued by agency personnel.

Maybe I am missing something here, but even though both Mike and I turned out to lead successful, integrated lives by most standards it seems to me that we could have benefitted from some process that explored—or tried to explore—our painful feelings. Was the absence of any such process an agency failing? Given the evidence of our psychological vulnerability at the time, I would have to say yes.

Granted, any psychiatric explorer certainly would have been confronted by our adamant refusal to discuss our feelings. Mike and I each adopted distinctive behavior patterns to avoid consciously revealing anything genuine about our emotional responses to our circumstances. Mike was consistently busy and evasive. As Chayet put it, "Michael seems carefree, active, and not particularly interested in discussion of anything other than play or group activities." Although she observed that Mike smiled much more than I and "appeared to have a rather cheerful . . . personality" he was often aggressive toward other children and very moody, resorting to hysterical crying jags "which take a great deal out of him."

I, on the other hand, usually impressed adults as being calmly communicative, "understanding of the situation in a manner that is rather mature for his age." Serkess observed as late as February, 1952, that "B. shows very few, if any, signs of emotional disturbance. He goes along pretty much on an even keel. I don't think I could ever recall hearing him ever cry at the Study Home. He seldom gets into any serious disputes or fights with children." One group worker put it like this: "Benjy reminds me of a little professor. He seems quite intelligent and likes to sit around and listen to adult conversation. He gets along well with the other children but usually will not join the other boys in any mischief. 'Crazy kids,' he calls them in adult fashion. He is cooperative, considerate, and seems much more sensible than any of the other children."

True to our respective behavior patterns, at the conclusion of our final meeting with Chayet, who had been our caseworker for a year, Mike couldn't wait to end the interview and join his friends at play. I, however, voluntarily stayed and conversed thoughtfully about my stamp collection. It appeared then to Chayet that I, "although somewhat passive in personality," was making a "successful adjustment" to my circumstances but that Mike had developed several symptoms, such as stuttering, poor schoolwork, and "regressive" behavior as a result of his emotional experiences and was "in need of help."

Apparently I was able to fool some of the people some of the time.

Understanding our evasive behavior was difficult, of course, for it usually amounted to: "I'm fine, go away," even in the worst—or especially in the worst—of times. For instance, only a few days after our second admittance to the study home following our mother's recommitment to the psychiatric ward, Chayet observed that I seemed "accepting" and "understanding" of the fact that our father would not be coming to visit us during the next weekend, while Mike "reveals an unconcerned attitude." But Mike and I must have needed our father at that traumatic time and been bitterly disappointed that we could not see him soon. Nevertheless, we easily fell into our traditional roles, adopting our calmly mature or carefree demeanors to conceal our emotional pain. Soon afterward, a group worker in the study home informed Chayet that she had "never heard either of the boys mention anything about their mother."

Mike and I probably believed we were successful in keeping our feelings of loss to ourselves, but chinks in our armor enabled agency personnel to discern and understand our vulnerability. The following anecdote is a case in point:

It is just after dinner, about seven o'clock at the study home. The children are engaged in an evening activity while Mike, Ben, and Chayet are in the course of a scheduled meeting in the "sewing room," a small and private room off the living room:

> Michael then inquired if worker has a pencil and when she gives him one announces that he is going to write a letter to his aunt. He looks at Benjamin inquiringly and Benjamin suggests that he begin the letter with something like, "I hope you are well". Michael continues writing letter by himself, only pausing to ask Benjamin how to spell "Argentina". After he finishes he reads back the following, "I hope you are well and come to see me. I am lonesome here and would like to go home soon. If you can, send me stamps of India and Argentina." When worker remarks that it really doesn't appear that he feels lonesome while at Study Home as he seems to be getting along very well and enjoying partaking in the activity groups, Michael grins but Benjamin looks rather solemn and it appears to worker from the boys' expressed attitude in this instance that there is present in them more of an awareness of the family separation than worker has realized but they decline to discuss it and their feelings seem to be accepting rather than disturbed ones.

During the "intake interview" with our father, on September 27, 1950, Benjamin Smith, Chayet's supervisor, having learned from Serkess that Mike and I had made no mention of our parents in our first two weeks at the Study Home, suggested that our behavior was rooted in our father's own need to avoid his pain regarding his wife and children. Smith wrote: "There may have been a great deal of blocking or non acceptance by the father of the idea of any possible problems concerning the boys as he continually glossed over questions in that area with 'They're both swell boys—healthy, well behaved.'"

I believe Smith's implication was that we boys had learned this strategy of denial at home. We had learned during our difficult years there that if we disavowed the pain associated with our mother's illness and our family's dissolution our troubles might really be of little consequence. For example, our father told Smith that Mike and I were aware that our mother was ill but "as she has had these periods before [he felt] they did not become too anxious or upset about the entire matter." That impression seems to have satisfied our father, but it would not have satisfied the agency's trained caseworkers.

Edward Portnoy, our next caseworker after Chayet, seems to me to have been especially able in understanding our behavior and sensitive in dealing with its consequences. "It is my impression," he remarked early in our relationship, "that B is not a very happy boy. I think that there is a great deal of passivity in him and a great deal of indecision . . . It is difficult to reach B . . . He does not relate too easily and is rather shy. He seems to feel that it is of the utmost importance to do things correctly and not to make a mistake."

Nowhere in the record is Mike's and my denial of our actual feelings more disturbing than in our response to our mother's death. Here is an excerpt from Portnoy's report of November 30, 1953, two days after our mother died in the Boston City Hospital. It is bitter evidence not only of the emotional cost of our "blocking behavior", but of our father's unwitting contribution to it. Portnoy's exhaustive report requires no further commentary from me.

> I received word . . . that Mrs. Gordon died during this past week-end [and] that the boys were told by their father to attend school this morning, which they did . . . At Bradshaw House, Benjy and Michael were both busy with arts and crafts and their behavior was not at all different outwardly. I spoke to B privately and expressed my shock and sympathy to him. He did not seem

to know from what his mother died, nor did he have anything much to say about her death. After I expressed my sympathy, he said, "That's all right" as though to comfort me. Since B did not know, I explained to him that his mother died of heart trouble. She had had a mild heart condition for some time and of course we did not know how serious this was. I wondered if he knew anything about the funeral and he said that he did not. He did not seem to want to talk any more about this and I made it clear to him that the agency would stand by him and Michael, and if there was anything that he wanted to talk to me about or ask me, he should not hesitate.

Michael seemed a bit more tense and nervous and tried to cover-up a good deal. He also did not seem to know what his mother died from and I told him so that he, as well as Benjy, would not have any fantasies, since they might imagine that perhaps she died from emotional difficulties . . . Michael also answered in monosyllables and seemed eager to return to his arts and crafts.

After discussion with my supervisor . . . it was felt that Mr. Gordon was being too protective of his children and was trying to cover up too much. It would be much better for them to face the reality of her death and to have had the funeral experience and the mourning experience (sitting shiva) as a catharsis, so that the children would be able to feel and to express their grief.

I, therefore, was able to find out from Benjy that his father was staying at his aunt's house . . . I was able to get in touch with Mr. Gordon that night and expressed my deepest sympathy to him and also our concern for caring for the children at this time, that the agency would be here to help them as well as himself. Mr. G told me that the funeral was held that morning and he did not feel that the children should attend . . . I told Mr. Gordon how I felt about having the boys with him at this time. I felt that he needed the boys and they needed him at this time and that he should include them in this period of grief . . . Mr. Gordon recognized this also and said he would send for them in the morning but would call them first. I also called M and B later and they said they would not go to school the following day, but instead would go to their aunt's house.

Mike and I spent the next day at Aunt Natalie's. I remember my father sitting on the couch in the dark living room, unshaven and in stocking feet. I remember a man bringing a basket of fruit to the door. That is all I am able to recall of the "period of grief" we shared with him.

Soon afterward Portnoy recorded Mike's response to his teacher's expression of sorrow on the day after our mother died: "I don't want to know anything about it."

Blocking behavior was "part of their problem," Portnoy told our father just after our mother's death. "They seem to cover up everything and it would be far better for them if they could express their feelings to somebody."

Weeks later Portnoy observed my behavior at Bradshaw House, saw it as an expression of feeling, and attempted to understand it in the context of my mother's death. Here is that entry. (Even now I sense his eyes upon me and feel just a little tempted to keep my secrets to myself. Did I feel then the presence of a mind that meant to invade my privacy? Perhaps, for my part in our conversation brings to mind the maxim about squeezing blood from stones):

B seemed to be in a rather exhilarated mood. He told me that he was feeling happy. I wondered why and he said that he really did not know, but then he pointed out that he played a trick on [another boy], taking his seat away. I wondered if he felt happy like this often and he told me "only once in a while."

I asked him how he felt otherwise, did he feel depressed? He said, "No, not depressed, just regular." I wondered whether he enjoys feeling happy like he does now or would he prefer feeling "regular". He told me that he would rather feel "regular".

Portnoy later recorded his "IMPRESSIONS" of this interview and another, related, incident:

More close observation will be made on Benjy. I have recently seen him at BH and notice that he looks rather depressed. He keeps to himself occasionally. Once I observed him alone trying to play a tune on the piano. Although it was supposed to be a fast, merry tune, he seemed to be playing it very slowly and methodically, so that it almost sounded like a funeral march. He told me that he liked to play the piano by ear. We will have to observe more in regard to the depressive and exhilarating moods that B seems to have. We wonder, perhaps, if there is some kind of identification with his mother who also had moods like this.

Whether or not Portnoy's hunch in this instance was correct, he certainly understood that it was one thing to define the problem and quite another to solve it. Portnoy tried hard to do both but, again, and despite his perceptivity, the agency made no attempt to reach behind the burdensome masks we wore. Only Portnoy's reports served to indicate the results such an attempt might have achieved.

Two months after our mother's death Portnoy attempted to discuss with Mike the possibility of leaving Bradshaw House and entering a foster home. He encountered only Mike's adamant refusal to continue the conversation. Portnoy said to Mike that he did not realize he liked Bradshaw House so much. Mike replied that it wasn't that he liked it so much, but just that he did not want to leave. "He then quickly changed the subject." In his next report Portnoy wrote of Mike: "It is very difficult for him to verbalize because he gets very anxious as soon as you hit upon something that may be meaningful to him."

My wife reminded me after she read this passage that it perfectly described Mike as an adult: maddeningly impossible to talk to regarding anything that existed beneath a significant issue's surface. When I reminded her that I might have been described as acting in an identical fashion, she said "Yes, but I won't let you." Unfortunately, Suzanne was not on the scene when I was twelve. Portnoy could have used the help.

Portnoy again probed behind my façade of equanimity a month after his abortive conversation with Mike. We were sitting across from each other in a restaurant. I was enjoying a slice of sponge cake and a glass of milk. Portnoy asked me "if there was much change in [my] feelings or if [I] could verbalize any feelings about [my] mother's death." He found me resolute in not discussing the matter and intent upon eating my cake:

> I asked B if his brother seemed to be worried in any way since his mother died. B said that his brother was not upset or worried about anything. I then went ahead and asked him if he was and he said no, he was not. I told him that sometimes it is good to be able to talk to somebody about things like that and B agreed with me. I said that before his mother passed away, he probably had the feeling that perhaps someday soon he

and Michael would be able to go home to his mother and father; however, now that his mother had passed away, he probably thinks that he won't be going home. He said that sometimes he thinks about that, but he was not able to elaborate at all.

Neither Portnoy nor any of our caseworkers was able to effectively penetrate our defenses despite the effort it must have cost them in the attempt. Many years later, as Mike lay dying in a Boston hospital, and having learned something from my wife, I suppose, about being in touch with my feelings, I tried to apologize to him for dismissively reacting to the two words he had offered me after our mother's death. He waved me off and shook his head. He declined to discuss it.

I cannot say that at seventy I am much better at summoning the will to discuss emotionally charged materials than I was at twelve. Indeed, I have marveled more than once at my current attempt to explore our troubled childhoods. I have sometimes sat frozen by sadness and unable to work on this memoir. Nevertheless, I am aware of my need to face the truth rather than to avoid it and, more to the point, to explore how the agency came to understand our emotional maladjustment despite its failure to treat it.

Solomon Lewenberg School Class of 1955

I AM CRUNCHED SECOND ROW CENTER,
DANNY IS 3 TO MY LEFT

Casework

My experience as an agency ward has convinced me that the agency's well-trained and caring caseworkers were the essential ingredients in its practice of child welfare. I believe that words like "astute" and "humane" are inadequate tools with which to characterize Edward Portnoy's response to Mike's and my emotional poverty at the time of our mother's unexpected death. Indeed, his response reached beyond us, for it necessarily included his counseling of our father at a difficult time for us all.

Although Portnoy's professional competence and sensitivity were remarkable they were not unusual. The reports submitted by our several caseworkers reveal that throughout our association with the agency they practiced a conscientious and highly personalized concern for our welfare. The first of hundreds of these reports, submitted by Leonard Serkess a few days after he drove us from the agency's office to the study home, modeled the thoughtful observation of our emotional status and the careful attention to our physical requirements demanded by Beatrice Carter of the agency's caseworkers as well as of other agency personnel.

> When I picked both boys up at the office, they . . . did not show too much outward anxiety. When we arrived at the Home I introduced them to the housefather who helped them to prepare for bed. By this time they

were expected at the Home, and clean beds had been prepared for them. From the start both boys proved to be self-sufficient. They were able to make their beds, dress themselves, and showed great ease in making friends among the children. So far, they have been very friendly with all the children and have established excellent relationships with the staff. They are well-behaved, well-mannered children. They present no problem in the area of eating and make no fuss at all about the food. Benj. appears to be the brighter of the two; Mike, as we know, stutters. Arrangements will be made for evaluation in this area . . . Mike is much more aggressive than his brother, B, and appears to be slightly duller. Both boys, because of the fact that they came with no clothes to speak of, were given complete wardrobes which seems to have had a very positive effect on them. They have not as yet talked about either their mother or their father.

The following verbatim excerpts from Mike's and my files illustrate the scope and substance of the caseworkers' responsibilities toward the children assigned to them. First, I present examples of their attention to our physical needs; then I offer examples of their sensitivity to our emotional needs. (Of course, the two bodies of material sometimes overlap). I also intend these extensive excerpts to illustrate my conviction that the caseworkers brought to their professional lives an appreciation of the individuality of the children they served and an admirable efficiency in satisfying their needs when they deserved to be satisfied. In any case, the excerpts certainly bring the reader face to face, and in meticulous detail, with the ordinary fabric of life in the agency's homes and with the caseworkers' daily concerns.

Life in the study home:

(1/23/51): "The following clothing bought for B. and M. during their (3-month, initial) stay at the S.H.: B.—1 jacket, 3 prs. pants, 1 suit, 5 shirts, 1 bathrobe, 1 pr. shoes, 1 pr. sneakers, 1 pr. slippers, 1 pr. overshoes, 1 pr. gloves, 1 hat, 1 tie.

M.—1 jacket, 1 suit, 3 prs. pants, 2 underwear tops, 5 shirts, 1 bathrobe, 1 pr. slippers, 1 pr. sneakers, 1 pr. shoes, 1 pr. overshoes, 1 pr. gloves, 1 hat, 1 tie.

(6/20/51): The following is a copy of M.'s report card for May and June: Conduct B; Effort B; English C; Music D; Arithmetic, E; Art D; Manual training D; Spelling A; Geography C; Reading D; Penmanship B.

(6/25/51) Worker made visit to S.H. to B. and M. She informs both boys that it has been arranged that they are going to Camp Kingswood for the first period. Both boys appeared to be markedly excited and enthused about the prospect of going to camp as they had never been before.

(9/6/51): Benjamin tells Worker of all the new things that he had learned to do at camp. He emphasizes the fact that he was allowed to swim in the highest waters there. Michael has just begun to learn how to swim and laughingly describes that he is able to swim under the water but cannot just stay on top.

(10/11/51): B. invited me up to his room to show me his stamp collection. B. discussed his stamp collection in a very intelligent manner, and it was quite obvious that he knew a great deal about geography.

(11/14/51): B. brought home the following report card: Conduct A; Effort A; Physical Ed A; Music B; Health Ed A; English B; Reading and Literature B; Spelling B; History A; Arithmetic C; Nature Study A; Geography A; Penmanship B; Art C; Manual training B.

(1/11/52): Dr. Margolis examined both boys and reported that one of B's eight year molars was missing. He also said that three of M's eight year molars were missing. Dr. Margolis recommended that both boys be examined at the Endocrine Clinic in order to determine if there is anything interfering with their growth process . . . The boys were bewildered because nothing was done to their teeth . . . B. remarked that they had to wait all that time for nothing and said, "After all that was said and done, a lot was said and nothing done." M. laughed and agreed with his brother. I told the boys that we would have lunch in town and that Mrs. Fox would buy them new shoes in the afternoon. Both boys seemed happier and thrilled over the fact that they would eat in a restaurant than that they were going to get new shoes.

(2/7/52): When B. and M. returned to the office with their shoes they immediately opened the boxes and showed them to me. M. asked if he could put them right on and wear them home. B. advised him against this and explained that they may get dirty and suggested that he wait until Sunday to show his parents his new shoes. M. obeyed B. and agreed to wait until Sunday to wear them. M. admires his brother and looks to B. for guidance. Before leaving I promised the boys that I would take them out for a good time. B. asked where I intended to take them and I told him that I intended to take them to the Science Museum. The boys were pleased to hear this and told me that they had never been there before.

Life in the study home annex:

(4/24/52): Visited the Study Home in order to bring M. to the B(eth) I(srael) H(ospital). M. was in a very cheerful mood and was eager to go. He said that Benjamin explained to him all about the examination and the only unpleasant part of the examination was the blood test. On the way to the hospital, M. explained that he liked the Study Home Annex much better than the Study Home in Brighton. There is a new group worker there by the name of Sheldon White that he likes very much. He takes them for bicycle rides, also swimming in the Brookline High School swimming pool . . . On the way home, M. described the ball game he attended at Braves Field, between the Red Sox and the Braves, with all the other children from the Study Home, as well as the boys from the Bradshaw Unit. He also spoke of the seder that was held at the Study Home.

Life in Bradshaw House:

(7/9/52): I asked them what they would like to do today. They didn't seem very enthusiastic and finally I suggested that perhaps we could go for a walk . . . We walked slowly to Blue Hill Avenue and entered a drugstore. They asked what they could have and I told them that they could have anything that they liked. They asked for a hot fudge sundae and although this cost a quarter I allowed them to have it and took one myself. The boys ate their sundaes with much relish and we left the drugstore to walk slowly back but on the way I told them that the sundaes did cost quite a bit and the next time we would probably have to restrict ourselves to a coke or something that would cost a little less. They agreed very readily to this.

(8/11/52): On this date, I interviewed both brothers together, briefly, at Bradshaw House . . . The interview was largely confined to the clothing needs of the children. Michael claimed that he needed sneakers badly and showed me one sneaker which was really torn so that it was almost impossible to continue wearing it. He has another pair of shoes which he can wear, not sneakers. However, he prefers to wear sneakers to play. He has one good pair of dungarees and a second torn pair. He has enough stockings and does not seem to be in need of other clothing. Benjamin claims that he has only one pair of stockings and needs this item badly. He doesn't seem, at present, in need of other clothes . . . They took me up to their room and I looked through their clothes together with them.

(2/9/53): I explained to B. that starting next week his Boy Scout dues would have to come out of his allowance and that I would not be able to give him an extra ten cent piece for this. I explained to him that if he were living at home and his parents gave him an allowance each week it would be up to him to decide what he wanted to spend it on. If he cared to join the Boy Scouts, then he would have to pay from his own allowance. I felt that this was only fair, since the other boys did not belong to Boy Scouts and if B. wanted any particular, extra activity like that he would have to pay for it out of his allowance. B. was able to accept this and said that he would not mind paying for it from his own allowance. B. was also very pleased since he gets $.50 allowance since his twelve year old birthday.

(3/24/53): Met B at Egleston Station after I wrote his teacher a letter asking that he be excused at 12:30 so that we could arrive for his shopping and visit to the BIH Eye Clinic. B needed a suit for Passover and he selected an attractive navy blue suit. We also bought him shoes, shirts, underwear and sox and a campus jacket. At the Eye Clinic, the doctor felt that B did not need any new glasses, that the eyeglasses he wore were adequate. He did mention that B did need an eye operation for cosmetic reasons.

(4/15/53): On this day I took M to the BIH Dental Clinic . . . There is no further dental treatment necessary and M was able to obtain his dental certificate which he was very proud of. However, the dentist did recommend orthodontia treatment which he felt M needed badly. I intend to make an appointment at the Tufts Dental Clinic for examination soon.

(5/1/53): M came running to me. He seemed to be quite concerned because I was supposed to write his teacher a note, saying that we would like him to go to the Theodore Roosevelt Jr. High School, the school his brother B is attending. As usual M was very anxious that I had forgotten to write this letter which he said he needed by Monday. I reassured him and as I was writing the letter for him, I talked to him about school. He said that he wanted very much to go to the Theodore Roosevelt Jr. High School, as his parents want him to go there and also because his brother goes there. He wants to take the academic course which I had discussed previously with him as being the right course for him since he was a bright boy and liked school and in case he ever decided that he wanted to go to college.

(5/1/53): I also discussed with Mr. G the fact that the doctor at the Children's Medical Clinic felt that B's circumcision wasn't performed very adequately since the foreskin still hangs over and is not pushed back . . . He felt that if the doctors, our agency and B wanted to have another circumcision, this would be alright with him . . . I impressed the fact that it was not necessary for B to have this operation, but perhaps in the future other boys may make remarks to him about this and wonder about his Jewishness. I told Mr. G that it was not important to do anything about this right now, it is something we can think about in our future planning.

(8/8/53): B was very glad to hear that he would be able to go to camp. The stitches were removed and his eye is looking considerably better . . . I forgot to mention that he received a card from the school committee notifying him that the Theodore Roosevelt School which he had been attending would be closed as a junior high school next year and he had been transferred to the Lewis Jr. High School. I do not feel that this Jr. High School would be good for Benj. and Michael Gordon, who was also supposed to go to the Theodore Roosevelt. The Lewis School is not in a very desirable location in Roxbury and I think the Solomon Lewenberg Jr. High School would be more adequate for B and M. Both boys would also rather go to the Solomon Lewenberg and I told them that I would find out about the transfer.

(8/11/53): I saw M and B off to Camp Chebacco at the YMHA in Roxbury. I gave them each 50 cents, money with which to buy postcards since they did not need money to purchase anything else at camp . . . B's eye looked much better . . . I forgot to mention that after the doctor first removed the bandage B seemed very pale . . . As we walked out a bus was approaching and B said that he would be able to go home with the bus. Of course I accompanied him. When we got to Mass. Station I asked if he wanted a coke and he said that he did . . . Suddenly without any warning, B threw up all over the place. After he threw up I told him that it was all right and that it was good that he was able to do this and that he needn't feel alarmed or ashamed about it.

(2/15/54): I spoke with M and B individually in regard to the new visiting schedule. M showed some reluctance but I explained to them the fact that we want the boys to have a hot lunch with us at BH. I also pointed out that at the Study Home visiting hours are only from 2 to 4 and we felt that the boys were staying away from BH too long. We would like them to be together and visiting hours would be from 2 to 7, unless something special comes up.

(3/24/54): On visiting the Solomon Lewenberg Jr. High School, I spoke with Michael's teacher . . . She felt that M is going down since his mother died. His conduct is not as good. She mentioned the fact that he usually has a very dirty neck and ears. However, M does dress neatly though. He is sensitive and blushes easily. He has a good relationship with his teacher . . . (She) also has Benjy in one of her classes and felt B should take a college course next year (which he will do) since he is a very bright boy and he is in with a rather "low group with little incentive this year and there is no competition for him." I spoke to both M and B about the school visit and M felt that he would try a little harder. I also arranged so that Martha Bernstein, the housemother, would help M with his French.

(4/13/54 thru 5/3/54): During this period Michael and Benjamin seemed to enjoy their Easter vacation very much. They seemed to play basketball and baseball quite a bit. They went swimming and to the movies and ball games. Since one of the boys got the chicken pox, the other boys did not join the Study Home in Brighton for the first Passover seder. However, they did have a seder at BH and enjoyed this.

Life in our first foster home:

(9/30/54): The mattresses came soon afterwards and Mrs. B. was very discouraged because the mattresses had a very peculiar odor of dampness ... The following day it was decided after conferring with my supervisor and the business manager and director of children's service that these mattresses would be returned to the warehouse and we would give Mrs. B. a certain amount of money for purchasing two new mattresses, but that she would pay the rest.

(11/1/54 thru 12/1/54): I worked out the boys' allowance with them, since it was a little different in a foster home. They each continued to get 50 cents for their allowance. In addition to this I gave them each 30 cents for movie money each week plus 25 cents for milk money. The boys did not need any carfare since they were right near their school. The total allowance came to $1.05.

Life in our second foster home:

(12/10/54 thru 1/24/55): The G boys stayed at BH until 1/10. I worked through this foster home placement with them very carefully, taking the boys out for a preliminary visit to Mrs. E.'s home and leaving them there for several hours. Transportation is not at all difficult and the boys seem to be impressed with the home. They did, however, want to continue at the Solomon Lewenberg Jr. High School in Dorchester. B. was going to graduate from this school in June; he liked the teachers and the other children and it would only take one hour in the morning to go to the Lewenberg from Winthrop . . . During this period I saw Mr. Gordon on an average of once a month. Reviewing his financial situation he told me that his net pay is $57 weekly. His rent is $45.75 and his telephone bill is $7.70, the gas bill is $4.30, electric bill, $1.75, carfare comes to approximately $12 a month and his food and cigarettes come to approximately $115 a month. This we worked out together plus the $4 a month for union dues; therefore, it would be difficult for Mr. Gordon to contribute more than $5 a week for each child at this time.

(2/1/55): I visited the E. home on the average of once a month during this period at which time I would also see the Gordon boys. Once a month also Mikey and Benjy would come to the office to see me . . . Mrs. E. found that laying out the allowance money and the haircut money for the boys interfered with her own budget because of the huge sum of money she would have to lay out. She felt that it would be easier if I would take care of the allowance money and the carfare money which I did. Each boy received $1.00 a week for allowance and this money was to take care of any recreation or school supplies that they might need.

(7/1/55 thru 8/19/55): Michael came into the office for pre-camp checkup . . . He was very happy that he was going to camp and did not seem to mind that his brother Benji would not go along with him, since he is too old for camp this year.

(8/19/55): I forgot to mention that I talked to Mr. Gordon before I left the Agency and he too was extremely pleased with the new foster home . . . I was able to work through with him an increase in his financial support

91

for the boys . . . It is important that arrangements be made for orthodontia treatment for Michael since he is badly in need of this . . . Both boys will need some clothing for the fall of 1955 and their clothing needs should be gone over with Mrs. E.

(8/19/55): I arranged with the Boston School Committee for this allowance and we did not have to pay tuition since ordinarily a child must pay tuition if he goes to a public school out of [the] town in which he lived. Both boys were very happy to complete the year at the Lewenberg School since they were fond of this school but both boys were able to accept the fact that they would transfer to the schools in Winthrop in September of 1955.

(12/27/55): Mikey told me that they had visited his aunt in Dorchester with his father last Sunday and had had dinner there. Mikey had done pretty well for himself this Chanukah, $5.00 from his father and $5.00 from his aunt. He was thinking that he would use it for some fishing gear specifically for a surf casting rod and reel so that he can go out with [his] housefather when he goes fishing. However, there seems to be some doubt as to whether a pair of ice skates wouldn't be a better choice in view of the weather. Mikey and I had quite a long talk about fishing and ice skating—it is certainly evident that he is a boy with many outdoor sporting interests.

(12/27/55): In a telephone conversation with Mrs. E. the problem of Mikey's feet was discussed. She indicated that Mikey's feet tended to perspire excessively and at times the odor was most noticeable. Although Mikey has foot powder and she reminds him to change his stockings each day this has still remained a problem which has been a source of much embarrassment to

Mikey as several of the children have remarked about it . . . I referred the matter to Dr. Paris in Chelsea and an appointment was made for Mikey to be seen at his office.

(1/18/56): Mikey told me that Mr. E. is active in the Jewish Community Center program for teenagers and that he is one of the leaders of the "tween club". The club sponsors quite a variety of activities, dances, games, chess, pool, etc. Mikey made a wry face at the mention of the dances and commented that the girls danced with each other for the most part which was all right as far as he was concerned. Since for him the best part of the dance was the food that is served.

(4/23/56): M. into office on this date. This was a rather short interview as M. seemed to have very little to say today. M. again had quite a load of books and talked somewhat about school today saying that he seemed to be getting along somewhat better in his Math. He seemed also to be rather pleased with the clothes he had gotten with Mrs. Fox. M. also was bubbling over with the first Red Sox game and described this in much detail.

(8/24/56 thru 7/29/57): The plan in regard to aptitudes testing in plans for college is that B. should be referred for a psychological evaluation the beginning of the school year and should also be referred to J[ewish] V[ocational] S[ervice] for scholarship assistance. During the summer B. has continued to work at Hamm's, however he has increased the number of days. At present he is working four days, Monday, Wednesday, Friday and Saturday and is saving most of his money. He is doing a lot of fishing, at times with M. and other friends.

(5/20/58): Letter received from B. detailing resources and expenses. Total estimated expenses, excluding clothing and incidentals, came to $888.50. Including $300.00 from his father, $125.00 in savings and $100.00 income as camp counselor this summer B. would have approximately $525.00 at the beginning of the semester . . . Ben into office in late August to arrange for payment of fees at the University of Massachusetts. Fees for 1st semester including tuition, room, board, activities, etc. amounted to $401.00, and a check for this amount was sent to the University of Massachusetts . . . I wished him continued success at school, asked him to send me a copy of 1st semester grades when they were sent to him.

(7/21/58): In the second week of July I had a call from B. who said that he had broken his glasses while on the waterfront at Camp Chebacco. Evidently he had dived into the water thus losing his glasses in the plunge. He said that he had gone to a Dr. Fine in Malden who gave him an eye examination and was going to replace his glasses. I got an okay from Mr. Grossner for payment of the optometrist's bill. This came to $23.00 including examination, lenses and frames. In July I had also sent a letter to B. stating that Mr. Grossner had given the okay on the agency's underwriting B.'s college expenses.

(January thru 5/11/59): I asked Mike how he had felt about it when I told him in September of arranging [orthodontic] treatment with Dr. Abrams. He said he hadn't liked the idea then, yet (on my inquiry) was afraid to tell me this! "I don't like to displease you—or people." I indicated to Mike that he should have felt free to tell me of his feelings. I went on to say that I had erred in not talking it over with him thoroughly, that I might anticipate his feelings. I later told Dr. Abrams of Mike's decision: accordingly, treatment was stopped.

(January thru 5/4/60): Mike's basketball activity has gone quite well with Mike getting the "most valuable player award" for his Center team . . . I asked him if he had been going out with girls at all, and he indicated that he was not going out with girls. One of the things that I would be concerned about Mike is his ability to relate heterosexually. This is a boy who does seem to prove his masculinity within the arena of sports and may have difficulty in establishing his masculinity on a heterosexual basis.

(1/7/62): [letter from Ben to caseworker Herman Steingraph]: Dear Mr. Steingraph: Greetings from the Berkshire foothills. I thought I'd better send this enclosed bill along before I lose it in the morass of material which is strewn about my room. Papers are near due and finals are approaching all-too-rapidly and I'm getting more depressed all the time. You'd think that after three years I'd be used to it. At any rate, I'll give you a call when I get in for the mid-semester break. Please take care of this little item for me. Thank you.

(3/1/62): I met with Mike for our last interview in January, 1962. Mike looked quite well, and he told me that he had recently received a $5.00 raise in salary from his employer. As in the past he felt that things were going along quite well at his place of employment. Mike was obviously quite reticent in this—our final interview—and I, myself, felt rather subdued and found it difficult at times to say anything.

These excerpts from our case files over a twelve-year period disclose the efforts of agency caseworkers to satisfy Mike's and my material needs. I believe they also reflect qualities of sound parenting. Our caseworkers maintained consistent contact with us (weekly or biweekly when we were young, less as we matured). One-on-one contact was the general rule, for the relationships required the caseworkers' appreciation of our particular characters. Caseworkers discovered our physical needs and did their best to satisfy them within reasonable limits that they set in consultation with us. In my experience honesty, generosity, caring, and commitment to our welfare characterized their efforts on our behalf.

Lengthy relationships with caseworkers frequently became personal. It is no accident that Edward Portnoy was my favorite, for in addition to his sensitivity and professionalism he was with me and Mike for nearly three years (October, '52 to August, '55) and through traumatic experiences. My parents frequently called attention to the personal interest he appeared to take in us. My mother wondered aloud after only four months of the relationship if she and my father would ever be able to thank the agency enough. "I told her that that was why our agency was here, to help people. She said, 'Yes, but such personal interest, I think it's wonderful." A month later Portnoy recorded: "Mrs. G. was extremely gracious and thankful and felt that I took a very personal interest in her sons." Again, several months later, while visiting me in the hospital before my eye operation, my mother marveled that Portnoy had arrived with ice cream and candy: "How good can you be, Mr. Portnoy." And as the agency began the process of moving Mike and me from Bradshaw House to a foster home my father "kept indicating to relatives that I have been like a father to his sons."

Herman Steingraph was with us even longer, although we saw him relatively infrequently in the approximately four years of our association. Mike, as I, was rapidly moving away from his ties to the agency in the final year of that period, but I believe their mutual reticence during their final interview reflected their sense of a shared experience and of a bond that had been meaningful to both of them. The flippant tone of my letters to Steingraph cannot conceal the affection and appreciation I felt for him.

Mike's and my relationships with the agency's caseworkers naturally involved issues of intense emotional weight. Caseworkers were trained to recognize and analyze evidence of that emotion, just as a concerned parent might take it upon himself to get to the bottom of his child's puzzling behavior. Consequently, our relationships with caseworkers throughout our years with the agency were sometimes highly charged in character. Excerpts from five years of case files—until the issue of our first foster home placement raised its head—illustrate the roles played by our caseworkers in our emotional lives.

Again, let the record speak for itself:

Life in the study home:

(10/19/50): For the past few weeks M. has been having a rather difficult time at the Home. Until several days ago, M. and his bro. B. had always partaken in all activities together. This past week on Sat., the children were divided into two groups for the purpose of activities, one group to go horseback riding and the other group bowling. M. and his bro. were placed in separate groups. B. made no comment about this but, before leaving, M. began to cry, to fight with the other children, and then spread himself out on the dining-room floor, kicked his feet, and refused to get up. He made quite a scene. It was by sheer physical force only that I was able to lift him up and take him out of the dining room. When I asked what had come over him, he cried and stated that he

97

wanted to go with his bro. The fear of separation was so great that I allowed him to go with his bro, B.

(11/15/50): B. is beginning to show some aggressive behavior. The other evening I observed his hitting one of the children of the S.H., for no apparent reason. He was not aware of my watching him. When I spoke to him about this, he stated that all of the children wanted to watch television, and she did not. I pointed out to him that television was not compulsory, and if she wanted to play by herself, this was no concern of his. His method of forcing her into the room indicated that there was some sex play involved, although I made no mention of this to him. I am observing him for some further display on his part.

(12/20/50): B. states that he hopes it will be possible for them to remain home but if his mother does not feel well they will be planning to return to the S.H. He has liked the S.H., it is the first time they have been in a "Jewish Home". He feels he is getting homesick, however.

(5/2/51): Worker . . . briefly speaks with group worker who describes her observations of both boys. M. is very active and athletic and often urges her to play ball with him. B. is more serious, he acts almost like a professor . . . She has never heard either of the boys mention anything about their mother and both seemed glad to return to S.H.

(6/19/51): Benjy . . . enjoys group activity and plays fairly even when his side is losing. Benjy alone of all the children seems appreciative of anything that he is given and of all the places he is taken.

Life in the study home annex:

(4/25/52): Mr. Smith, Supervisor, informed that Benjamin and another boy were to be moved to Bradshaw House that day, from the Study Home Annex. M. acted in an indifferent manner but B. felt very bad. He became hysterical and locked himself in the bathroom and refused to come out . . . I was left alone with B. and I talked to him. He calmed down after a while and came out of the bathroom. When I assured B. that I would not force him to go to Bradshaw if he did not want to, he said that he was willing to come with me to the agency to talk the matter over . . . At the agency . . . Mr. Smith called Mrs. Gordon and B. also expressed his feelings to his mother over the phone. Mrs. Gordon was against separating the boys and said she would rather take them home again rather than to allow this to happen. Mr. Smith then took into consideration the chance of endangering the health of their mother and sent B. back to the Study Home to stay with his brother.

(5/24/52): The boys talked about the activities of the Study Home and B. reminded me of the victory he won over the agency by refusing to move and M. was amused by this.

Life in Bradshaw House:

(10/29/52): Today the Supervisor of the Units [Leonard Serkess] announced to the boys that the Cisco Kid and Pancho were going to visit the Brighton Home and that he would take all the boys there right after school tomorrow. M. became very much upset because for some reason he felt that he would not be able to go . . . I told Mike that I would like to talk this out with him so that I could help him so that he too would be able to get out from school on time and see the Cisco Kid. However, M. began to cry and would not come near me. He started to run away from me and whenever I would come downstairs to talk with one of the boys he would peer around from the corner and try very hard to keep out of my way. I told him finally that I would not be able to help him unless he would want to talk this out with me. He finally told me that sometimes he has to stay after school, since his teacher is trying to help him with some of his work. I asked M. why he kept avoiding me and running away from me when I only wanted to find out why he felt he would not be able to get out of school on time . . . He told me that he always did this and he does not know why. I pointed out to him that I was his social worker and that I was very much interested in him and helping him whenever anything was bothering him or when he felt discouraged he could talk with me about this and perhaps we both could reach some understanding . . . I told M. that I would visit his teacher the following day and talk with her. [After a long conversation with the principal and a sympathetic teacher] arrangements were made so that the Bradshaw House Director would pick M. up . . . on the way to the Brighton Study Home to see the Cisco Kid.

(11/10/52): I spoke with B about the fact that he used to visit his mother after school at the beginning of this year. I wondered why he did this. He felt that the reason why he did this was because he and Michael thought they would be going home soon and, therefore, they visited their mother. However, now he accepts the fact that they are not going home for some time and he, therefore, will not visit his mother. I pointed out that while the boys live at Bradshaw House it is better if they visit their parents on Sundays during visiting hours.

(11/19/52): I met Michael and Benjie near their schools to take them shopping for winter coats. M had been the first to arrive and he . . . spoke to me about the shopping trip and the type of coat that he would get. He told me that he did not want a long, storm coat but rather a short jacket with fur collar. A stray cat happened to be nearby and M stopped to pat it. He was very affectionate to this cat and held it in his arms, stroking it and telling me that he likes cats very much. However, he does prefer dogs. After B arrived we went on our way to meet the purchasing agent. I also took them into a Howard Johnson's and both boys devoured a hot fudge sundae with much gusto.

(2/6/53): B is a rather bashful boy. He seems to be on the verge of smiling while I am talking to him. I told him that I visited his mother and father and told him how nice they were and how well his mother was able to prepare the table for snacks. B said that she always does this nicely . . . As I spoke with B I noticed that he got up out of his chair and walked behind me as though talking to me face to face produced too much pressure for him and he felt "on the spot". I asked him if he wouldn't rather sit down where I could see him, since he continued talking to me but was moving around and had maneuvered to sit behind me. He said that he would surely like to sit in front of me which he did.

(6/5/53): M has been having some temper tantrums recently according to the housefathers. He is also acting in a "persecutory manner" which he sometimes does. I brought M and Benjy bathing trunks and jerseys. Almost immediately M did not like one of his trunks which were silver in color. Actually it was a very attractive bathing suit which the other boys and B liked very much, but M seemed to feel that he would look funny in it and he did not like it. I told him that I could change the bathing suit for him if he really didn't like it and he said never mind he didn't want it. He ran out of the room saying that he would not take his allowance at this time. Since one never gets anywhere when one tries to follow M during one of his temper tantrums, I did not follow him and I thought that I would give him his allowance next Monday when perhaps he would be in a more accepting mood.

(6/15/53): Met Michael and Benjy at Egleston Station to take them to Tufts Dental Clinic. M seemed to be rather anxious. He kept asking me what they would do to his teeth today and I assured him that they were only going to look at his teeth to see if orthodontia was necessary and would let us know when they would start . . . He seems to be very sensitive and one must be very careful when one talks to him since he feels hurt very easily. He and Benjy were both very clean and nicely dressed and they seemed to get along well with each other.

(9/21/53): Mrs. Gordon telephoned to thank me for allowing M and B to go home for the Yom Kippur week-end. She told me that she had "a wonderful, delightful" weekend with the boys. She wondered if they would be able to spend other week-ends at home. She told me that she had an app't at Briggs Clinic the following night and she would be going with her husband. I told her that where the children are in placement at BH, we could not ordinarily allow them to go home on week-ends. However, if she thinks she is feeling better and would like to have the children home a little more, perhaps we will allow this if it is recommended by the doctor whom she sees at the Briggs Clinic. I later telephoned the Briggs Clinic to discuss this with them.

(12/14/53): M continues to be a rather anxious lad, who tries to cover up by asking all sorts of questions. For instance, while I was at BH on 12/14, he wondered why I was there so early since I usually came later in the afternoon. As I have mentioned before, M always fears a new change and anticipates the anxiety that such a new situation or change might bring about in him. Perhaps he has good reason to feel this way in view of his past history, going to relatives to Study Home, back home again, only having to return again to Bradshaw House because of his mother's recurring illness, and particularly in view of his mother's unexpected death.

(1/28/54): M's report card read as follows: conduct A, effort A, physical education B, music A, health education B, English C+, history A-, French C-, math C, general science B, geography B, penmanship B-, art B-, industrial art B. It is interesting that he received a C—in French, since this is a subject that his mother always used to want to help him with. I will have to find out some more about why M does not do as well in French as he does in other subjects.

(3/11/54): I forgot to mention that B was on the honor roll in school during the months of January and February. He received a huge certificate . . . and was extremely happy about this. Mr. G. was also very proud. However, Michael Gordon did not do so well . . . M's grades in French have gone from a B—to a D. I still feel that somehow this is tied up with his mother's death, since she would help M in the course. M had a tremendous amount of feeling and was embarrassed about this, even hesitating to show me the grade. Some of the boys teased him about the D, although some of the boys certainly got more failing marks on their report cards. I tried to reassure M, saying that we all

cannot do well all of the time and most of us receive a
D once in a while. He seems to feel that he will never get
on the honor roll as his brother did. I reassured M and
encouraged him and told him that I would definitely
go up and talk with his French teacher and see what
we can do to bring his mark up. M wants to continue
taking the French course and perhaps Mrs. Bernstein,
the housemother, will be able to tutor M in this course.

(3/19/54): I accompanied Michael to Tufts Orthodontia
Clinic for an appointment with Dr. Margolis, the director
there. Michael seemed to be quite anxious again, asking
me all sorts of questions wanting to know exactly what
the doctor was going to do, whether he would start
treatment and whether he would wear a night brace or
a day brace. He wants to have orthodontia treatment.
He prefers not to wear braces during the day, although
I explained to him that this may be necessary. He then
said that he would not mind.

(4/12/54): According to the housefathers and the other
boys at BH, M is an outstanding athlete, particularly
in baseball. This seemed to mean very much to him.
However, it was felt that M was a very poor loser. He
is very irritable, particularly when somebody on his
team makes a mistake. He flies off the handle easily. The
new housefather, Babe Yosselivitz, who is captain of the
Brandeis Basketball Team, is trying to help M to have
better sportsmanship. Therefore, it was not felt that M
was ready for outside group activity . . . He was very
determined to join the Little Leaguers and said that he
was going down there for practice on Saturday morning,
regardless of what the rule at BH was. I told him that I
did not make the rules, the only thing I could do was to
help him see that since he was living at BH, he had to
cooperate and participate in the program there. M told

me that his father wanted him to join the Little League
and he was going to do this.

(5/3/54): I did discuss with both M and B that I would
like them to have psychological tests done with Dr.
Platt. They both knew Dr. Platt, since both boys were
tested about two years ago. I felt that this was important,
since it would be helpful in planning for both boys and
particularly to help us determine what course they
should take in high school. Actually, I would like to
know what the tests show, particularly in Michael. Both
boys agreed to be tested . . . I told B that I understood
he did not like to stay out from school, but this was
important.

(6/16/54): After the testing situation, I took Benjy out to
lunch. He seemed to enjoy light talk about the restaurant
we were eating in and the food he was going to order . . .
He did not mention the testing situation at all and I
finally asked him how things went. He told me that the
testing was okay; Dr. Platt had informed me that he had
discussed foster home placement with Benjy who broke
down and cried. I tried to clarify to Benjy the reason
for Dr. Platt asking these specific questions, because
sometimes a boy may have a lot of fear or worry around
this and, very likely, I stated, most boys do masturbate
once in a while and this was not bad for them, in that it
does not do any harm.

These and scores of other entries in our files reveal the frequently
personal nature of our relationships with caseworkers as well as
the breadth of their emotional content. Couple these relationships
with the quasi-parental bonds we frequently established with our
housefathers, housemothers, and other agency personnel and
our mighty resistance to the agency's determination to move us
from group care at Bradshaw House to a foster home can be no

mystery. Edward Portnoy, Frank O'Rourke, Martha Bernstein, Mrs. Roshelitz—they cared about us and took care of us. Bradshaw House was our home away from home and we saw no reason to displace our parents once again. Given this context, the agency's attempt to move Mike and me to foster care would require all the sophistication in our caseworker's arsenal.

"Foster Families"

I wouldn't leave Bradshaw House no matter who said I should, even Martha, even Mr. Portnoy. I wouldn't. I wouldn't leave Danny and Gerry or even Norman. I wouldn't leave the housefathers and Mrs. Roshelitz. I liked it there too much to leave. I liked sitting around the long table in the dining room for meals, all the kidding around and the time Frank threw a hot baked potato at Stuart when he swore. I liked playing chess with Frank or Danny, the feeling of being quiet and intent and apart from everything else in the world. I liked the excitement of fishing with my pals for barbed hornpout near Houghton's Pond, the patient waiting for that electric tug on the line while the sun pressed hard on my back. I liked the freedom I felt when I walked by myself all the way to Grove Hall on that scorched August afternoon, a big bag of cherries and a package of cream cheese my lunch and no one to scold me very much for doing so. Why should I leave my home for another I did not know no matter how nice the people? I wouldn't.

I had locked myself in the bathroom at the top of the stairs and, yelling and crying, refused to come out. It had been a long time. I imagined Martha crouching on the other side of the door, her head at just the same level as mine as I sat on the toilet cover and leaned forward toward the door and Martha's voice, only a thin wooden panel between us. I refused to hear what I didn't want to hear but knew I must, knew it was inevitable.

"Benjy, you know we want what's best for you," Martha said, "You can't stay here forever. You're lucky to have a family that wants you to live with them. Mr. Portnoy says they're nice. I bet you'll be happy there. And they live right near your school. You'll be able to walk there. It'll be alright, Benjy. You'll see. Come on out. Supper's soon."

I heard her rise and leave and there was silence. I sat on the toilet with my arms crossed and my hands holding my shaking self and waited for someone else to come but no one did. Later, when I unlocked the door and opened it and walked slowly downstairs it was dark outside and my supper was still warm in the oven.

*　　*　　*

The lady did the talking while her husband drove. I sat with Mike in the back and listened to her tell us that her husband sold toys. He kept many of them in his garage, she said, turning her head and looking over her seatback at us. She said: "Some of those toys will be coming into the house soon" and I knew I couldn't trust her. I didn't care about their stupid toys. I didn't care about Chanukah or Christmas. I didn't want to be there and they couldn't make me want to be there. I knew this was not going to work. I would be back at Bradshaw House. I would be a Bradshaw House Bum again. They'd see.

One day she was working in the kitchen, baking. The kitchen was full of sunlight and sweet smells. I wanted to ask about the baby she was expecting but I didn't know how to and I had nothing else to say to her. I stood in the doorway and watched and then I asked her for a piece of the dark chocolate that lay on the yellow counter. She said it was not for eating like that, that I would not like it, that it was bitter. I knew better than that. It was chocolate, wasn't it? and I asked her again for a piece. She said o.k. and gave me a thick square piece and I took it out to the back yard and I bit into it and I spit it out onto the grass. It was bitter and I was angry.

There was a child, maybe two years old. I was sitting on my bed, my feet on the floor, and I was doing nothing. She came in and stood close and in front of me and looked up at me expectantly, and I put my hand on her small blonde head and pushed her away. She came back, soundlessly, and I pushed her away again. She returned, looking at me wonderingly with round blue eyes. I pushed her away and she returned and her mother came into the room and looked at me, saying nothing, and picked up the baby and left me alone and within days I was back at Bradshaw House because she could not trust me, she told me. I was glad to be back but there was a bitter taste in my mouth that had not been there before.

*   *   *

We were sitting on a wooden bench in a little alcove, a breakfast nook the blonde lady called it, in a house in Winthrop. Mr. Portnoy told us on the way to the house that the lady wanted to meet us and talk to us before she decided to take us into her family and she was going to cook supper for us and talk to us while we ate. He told us that we should think about living there and that he thought we would like it just fine. When we got there we could see the water and the sailboats right across the street and we could hear the halyards clinking against the masts and the seagulls were flying right over the house and crying sadly the way seagulls do. The lady met us at the door and Mr. Portnoy said he would be back later and we went with the lady through a porch that was all glass and into the house and then into the kitchen.

We sat on the bench that like the walls was made of shiny wood with dark brown spots all over. The table had a smooth red top and it reflected the light from the lamps on the walls. The lady said supper was coming soon and that we could talk while we waited for it. I didn't know if I should fold my hands on the edge of the table or keep them on my lap and while she talked to us I tried both ways.

The lady sat down on the bench across from us. She asked us our names and she told us her name and her husband's name and her children's names. She had three children and she said I would be the oldest if I lived there with them and that if I really wanted to I could travel all the way to Mattapan to finish junior high school although there was a perfectly good junior high school in Winthrop and I said I really did want to travel to Mattapan because that was where my friends were and I didn't mind the rides on the bus and the trains and the streetcar and she said it was a long way but it was fine with her and I could do my homework on the way.

We talked about the Red Sox but she said she didn't know much about baseball and she asked us some questions about it and we told her the answers. She said she should mention Penny, too, and that he would wake me up in the morning if I slept near the window because he wanted to get in and he would climb up the pear tree behind the house and jump onto the roof and come to the window and scratch it and if I let him in I would have a friend forever. I thought it was funny to have a cat that was your friend and I laughed and told her about Toastie and how she had come to me when I was in bed to show me that during the night she had had kittens in the laundry basket in the closet.

When the lady gave us supper we could tell that it was a stew with meat and vegetables but the meat was very tough. We didn't want to say anything or hurt her feelings and we chewed and chewed and we said that it was very good when she asked us how we liked it and she said that was good and she sat with us and smiled a lot while we ate. We ate everything on our plates and when she asked us if we wanted more we said no we were filled. We had vanilla ice cream on brownies for dessert and then Mr. Portnoy came and we said thank you to the lady and she said it was a pleasure to meet us and she walked out to the car with us and we all waved goodbye.

It was still daylight and the seagulls were still flying over the water and the sailboats and the house and they were beautiful to see, so graceful and free. In the car Mr. Portnoy asked us how it went and we said good. We drove back to Bradshaw House that evening but soon we were living in Winthrop.

Foster Home Placement

Several members of the agency's staff met in late June, 1954, at a kind of summit conference intended to explore the difficult task of moving me and Mike from group care to a foster home. The agency was committed to its conviction that such a move was in our best interest. However, after a four-month attempt to persuade us to see the situation as it did they continued to face our fierce resistance to the proposition. Doctor Platt presented the results of our recent psychological examinations and emphasized our suspicion of others' motives and our fear of change. He then succinctly defined the challenge that faced the gathered staff members: "Benjie, like Michael, insists he will not leave Bradshaw House until his father is ready to take the boys home. He will not consider foster home placement as a stepping stone to eventual return to his own home."

Platt emphasized the necessity of our father's involvement in the process of bringing us around. "I would again like to suggest, he said, "that the father somehow be involved in planning around the boys. I gather from speaking to Benjie, as I did to Michael, that Mr. Gordon seems to play a rather passive role in planning for the boys."

Although at the time there was no reason to believe that Mike and I would soften our opposition to a foster home placement, within three months intensive casework with our father would allow the agency to reach its goal.

The issue of our placement had first surfaced during Portnoy's February 12, 1954, conversation with Estelle Cross, his supervisor in the agency's foster care department. Perhaps, they agreed, a little more than two months after our mother's death, we should think about foster home placement." Although Mike and I had lived in group homes for almost four years, far longer than appropriate by agency standards, foster home placement had not been considered because of the possibility that Mike and I would return to our parents. Our mother's sudden death had dramatically altered that perception and Portnoy and Cross agreed that foster home placement "might be better for them," as Mike and I were "unable to get much more out of institutional living." From that point on, until our first foster home placement more than seven months later, the agency worked assiduously to bring about the transition everyone except Mike and I seemed to approve as the best course of action for our welfare. All continued to believe, as well, "that the BH setting could serve other boys more at this time than it helps to serve the Gordon boys who have certainly had the group setting far too long."

From the start it was apparent that a successful placement would require significant casework with our father, who soon accepted Portnoy's invitation to come into the office to discuss the proposed step. Portnoy explained that Mike and I had been living in group homes for several years, that we were ready for a move away from institutional living, that foster parents could give personal attention to us that we could not find at Bradshaw House, that he would be able to know the foster parents and visit us just as before, that the agency would do nothing abruptly, and that Mike and I would visit the proposed foster home before any placement was arranged.

Our father was apprehensive and Portnoy observed that his eyes welled up with tears. Wouldn't we feel as if we were just being "shoved away?" Not so, Portnoy answered. He would explain to us that the move was for our own good and that this was a plan meant to help us. He insisted that our father's participation in this move was important, for we needed him to play a central role in our lives.

Finally our father agreed. "He saw that this would be good for his boys, and he felt that this plan must be interpreted to them and should not be done abruptly." He was, apparently, on board.

Three days later Portnoy calmly presented to Mike and me, individually, the possibility of our moving to a foster home. "I told M sometimes a boy has lived in an institution for a very long time and has gotten a lot out of it and it is time for him to go ahead to take a step ahead and to move into a foster home." Mike leaped from his chair, started to cry, and ran from the room shouting that he was not going to leave. Housemother Martha Bernstein reminded Portnoy that there was no catching Mike when he was in such a mood.

Portnoy tried me next, knowing me to be, "of course . . . much more stable and calmer" than Mike. The agency cared for me, he explained. They all loved me and wanted to help me. I would get personal care from fine foster parents. He would continue to be my social worker. We would go to the same school. We would see our father every Sunday. The choice, he said, was ours.

I had been sitting absolutely still, looking at the floor, throughout Portnoy's words of encouragement. When he asked what I felt about "all this" my response was no less hysterical and theatrical than Mike's. I began to cry. I jumped up, grabbed my jacket and rushed screaming from the room: "I'm not going to leave! I'll run away!" Within moments I had locked myself in the bathroom and threatened never to come out.

Martha, round and motherly, managed to settle Mike and me down and before Portnoy left that evening he had explained to us that no one was going to force us to go to a foster home.

That stance was confirmed soon afterward when Portnoy met with Dora Margolis, Dr. Platt, and Cross. Portnoy shared his opinion that it was too soon after our mother's death to lose the security we enjoyed at Bradshaw House. "It was felt that through working out the boys' feelings about why they do not want to leave BH, it would help them start to express feelings around loss and security."

Two weeks later our father and Portnoy talked again in Portnoy's office. Mike and I, our father said, had never mentioned to him the subject of foster home placement . . . He agreed to speak to us about a foster home's being good for us. Portnoy made it clear that he should mention their conversation, lest Mike and I suspect a conspiracy. "At all times," he counseled our father, "the truth and the nature of our appointments should be interpreted to the boys."

Portnoy talked to me soon afterward about my reaction to his introducing the subject of foster home placement. I told him I did not know why I wanted to stay in Bradshaw House, but the fact was that I did and I didn't want to talk about it any more.

Three months later our father and Portnoy spoke again, but in all that time our father had never mentioned to us the subject of foster home placement. Portnoy found this "interesting" and suggested that "perhaps Mr. G should ask the boys why they are attached to Bradshaw House and make them feel that he is aware of the discussion they had with me." The project had stalled, but had not gone away; the agency was waiting for our father to play an active role in bringing us around. In fact, the agency's consulting psychiatrist, Dr. Joseph Sabbath, with whom Portnoy met on a weekly basis regarding all the boys at Bradshaw House, suggested that Portnoy's priming our father with things to say regarding our future might be a necessary strategic tool in the agency's overall approach to the problem.

These and other discussion points were the subjects of the late June summit conference attended by a large cast of characters. In addition to Portnoy, Dr. Sabbath, and Dr. Platt were Dora Margolis, Director; Estelle Cross, Supervisor; Leonard Serkess, Director of the Units; and Jeannette Alpert, Art Instructor. There was no shortage of man-hours expended on the future of the Gordon boys, but nothing had changed. There were no reservations about the consensus that Mike and I needed to be in a foster home as preparation for a future in which we would live within a family. Dr. Sabbath cited our extreme reaction to Portnoy's suggestion of a foster home placement as insecurity stemming from our mother's death. All agreed that when the parents were expecting to take their sons home it was difficult to contemplate foster home placement; now, however, the parent must participate in the planning for that move.

Securing that participation, however, continued to be elusive. In mid-July Portnoy met again with our father, who now did not think foster home placement to be such a good idea. He had asked Mike and me why we liked BH so much. We had told him "that [we] liked all the kids and the staff there. [We] also enjoy the activities." But "this was not enough," Portnoy insisted, to justify our opposition to the agency's decision. Then our father suggested that he take us home, that we would be able to shift for ourselves and he would probably be able to make supper for us. Portnoy discouraged this line of thought. It would be very difficult for us to adjust to the frequent absence of a parent, he explained. We needed familiarity with family living and a foster home would provide that. Portnoy again emphasized that the plan to place us in a foster home should come from him as our father, that he should talk to us and tell us that he had been thinking about our future and what is best for us.

After considering Portnoy's argument our father agreed again that foster home placement was necessary. "Mr. G. said he will talk to M and B about separation from BH gradually and try to show them how much to their advantage a foster home would be." Afterward, Portnoy wrote in his notebook: "IMPRESSION: Mr. G is very cooperative and agreeable to show M and B he is with us in this plan. We wonder about his hostility underneath."

Two weeks later our father was in Portnoy's office again. He told Portnoy that he had been gradually discussing foster home placement with us but that we did not want to talk about it. When we next visited him in Roxbury he brought the subject up again as something that would be good for us and, Portnoy recorded, "[we] were able to express to him that [we] would rather go home with him." Portnoy asked what his feelings were about that. "He thought that he could get them off to school in the morning and then at night he could cook supper for them . . . Of course he would prefer this if his boys were older." Portnoy again discouraged the idea and repeated his conviction that we, just thirteen and twelve, needed full time care. Since our father remained hesitant about the whole situation, Portnoy arranged that he speak to his supervisor.

Cross also discouraged any plan to bring me and Mike home. Maybe in five years, but now we were too young. "It would be good for [us] to come home from school and have somebody greet [us] and talk to [us] about school and answer [our] questions and give [us] a glass of milk." She spelled things out for my father: We needed preparation for family life, needed the personal attention a foster home could give us. The foster parents' care of us would be overseen by the agency. The foster parents work for the agency. They like children. The agency would be doing us no favor by allowing us to stay at Bradshaw House. By the close of the interview our father expressed his relief. He was again reassured about the advisability of foster home placement for Mike and me.

But Portnoy found himself still working through our father's resistance toward foster home placement when they next met two weeks later. He "continually tried to get to Mr. G's feelings." Told that we remained silent concerning the issue, Portnoy stressed that we had to feel that our father was convinced that a foster home was right for us. In an attempt to fathom his reluctance to fully engage in the plan, Portnoy "asked him if he felt that perhaps he wasn't doing enough" for us. There wasn't much he could do, he answered, as he had given up as premature the idea of bringing us home. Portnoy asked if he had told us this. No, he hadn't, but he promised to explain to us that he could not care adequately for us, and that foster parents would help him do that.

"I tried to show Mr. G how important he would still be in his sons' lives," Portnoy recorded. Our father "seemed to like the idea that everything would be the same, that he will be able to arrange for [Mike's] bar mitzvah and will be able to take his sons out and visit them. He will tell his sons that this is what they need and he wants them to do this." Portnoy then reassured him about the foster parents. It was true that they were paid, he explained, but they like and care for children and are closely supervised by the agency. "He seemed to appreciate this."

With our father again apparently on board, he and Portnoy agreed that the move should be made in early September, before the school year began. Our father told Portnoy that he would gradually make it clear to us that we would be moving in September.

Our father's reluctance and our own had apparently been finally overcome. Mike and I no longer fought the move to a foster home once we sensed what passed for our father's firmness regarding the virtues of that step. We both approached it as if our resistance had never been. If our father thought it right for us, we would give it a try. We were anxious, however, that a home be found nearby so that we could continue to attend Solomon Lewenberg.

Before that, however, there was camping in New Hampshire and a trip to New York City to enjoy.

After the intensive casework with our father, the essential prologue to our foster home placement, our initial experience of a foster home was a painful failure. The intended pre-placement visit to the couple's house fell through the cracks, but even then I knew—or felt—that these particular "parents" were not right for us. We knew that they were expecting a baby of their own, that they already had a two-year-old girl, and that despite their volunteering to undertake the responsibilities of foster parenting they were focused on their own family rather than on our intrusive, angry, suspicious, fearful, adolescent selves. I could not have articulated these feelings at the time, even if I had been disposed to do so, but I know they were simmering in me and quickly became identified as "resentment" by my foster mother.

It sorely tests my credulity now that the agency could have considered the Bs appropriate parents for us. I believe that the need, as the agency perceived it, to move us from group living circumstances outweighed any consideration that this particular placement was ill-advised. On the other hand, finding a family willing to take in two children must have been exceedingly difficult. That level of difficulty, I think, contributed to the first attempt's failure, rather than any disregard for our needs. In fact, the agency's later ability to find a second family willing to take us in suggests to me a heightened indefatigability on our behalf. Nevertheless, this complex experience—as well as others I will consider—leads me to infer that the urgency to find suitable foster families occasionally led the agency to be too easily satisfied with some that were inappropriate for the children they were intended to serve.

Our files indicate that everyone initially tried to make the new arrangement work. Portnoy accompanied us to our new home where we were warmly greeted by Mrs. B and her daughter. Mike had wanted to bring a favorite cat from Bradshaw House, but settled for care of the B's parakeet. "The boys were very pleasant," Portnoy noted, and "busied themselves unpacking." Arriving home from work, Mr. B "lost no time in making friends" with us. Soon we told Mrs. B that at mealtimes we wanted to set and clear the table, as we had done at Bradshaw House. Mrs. B took us grocery shopping and bought our favorite breakfast cereals. When she returned from the hospital with her baby, she reported to Portnoy, we were "elated" and enjoyed looking at the baby and playing with her.

But soon problems appeared, frequently revolving around food. Mike and I were blatantly antagonistic. We sat down at the kitchen table and chanted in unison, "We want to eat; We want to eat." We demanded to know what was for dinner the next day. I asked Mrs. B when we were going to have steak. I intentionally clattered the silverware into its drawer. Mrs. B complained to Portnoy that we were consuming "huge quantities" of food. We would eat many slices of bread and always want more. One Saturday afternoon she served franks and beans. Mike and I "really stuffed" ourselves and were sick afterward but, she added, "they would never admit to her that they were."

Mrs. B believed that our father was at the root of this behavior. She overheard nightly telephone conversations in which we responded to his questions about our diet with meticulous descriptions of our meals. She told Portnoy that she thought I came away depressed from those conversations. Portnoy must have realized that our father's own equivocal attitude toward foster home placement was prejudicing us against the Bs. He talked at length with our father, reassured him that we were being well-fed, and limited telephone conversation to two evenings a week.

Our almost palpable antagonism regarding food soon expressed itself as a general distrust and tension between us and our foster mother. By early December she "felt that things were not going along well at all." She remarked to Portnoy "how resentful B seems to be." Issues concerning a lost container of ant killer, a broken lamp, stolen cookies, a pack of cards, and burnt bacon that she had allowed me to cook all filled the household with a poisonous atmosphere. She reported that Mike was easier to live with than I, but "it has gotten so that she is almost afraid to trust B in the house," even to the point that she feared I might hurt her two-year-old. She did not trust me to get her a glass of water "because maybe he would put hot water in it or something else."

In response to the situation's gravity Portnoy talked with Mike and me individually. Mike answered his questions with monosyllables. "I told him," Portnoy reported, "that things were not going along right and I would not be able to help him if he continued to keep all his feelings bottled up within him without letting me know what was bothering him." In a rare moment of transparency Mike choked back his tears and was able to tell Portnoy that he was not happy there. He did not like Mrs. B. She was too strict sometimes and made him do a lot of things like go to the store. He "was aware of the fact that most of the difficulty was with B."

I cried quietly while I spoke with Portnoy, who wondered why I had never told him of my unhappiness in my new home. "I was trying to make it work out right," I said, but "she accused me and did not trust me." We discussed the issues she had brought up and I explained them. I would have told her about the broken lamp but she was resting; I would not hurt the child . . . I liked her. During our lengthy conversation Portnoy assured me that "it was good" for me to be able to tell him how I felt about my foster home. He must have been gratified to have successfully moved both Mike and me to discuss our feelings.

Portnoy and Cross visited the home together. They arranged with Mrs. B that Mike and I be required to do fewer household tasks.

Portnoy talked to me about this adjustment and I said I wanted "to give it a try," for I felt I was not ready to live with my father.

I did try, however ineffectively, and so did my foster mother. She told Portnoy that I was often crying in my room but would pleasantly greet her when I emerged. She had a long talk with her husband and they agreed that she might have been "a little harsh and hostile." Perhaps, she thought, the family might be stronger if we boys did our homework at the kitchen table rather than behind our room's closed door. However, the apparent underlying motive for her sensible suggestion must have made Portnoy and Cross doubt the likelihood of effective change on her part: we were wearing out the wool of our blankets, she complained, when we lay on our beds to read. Nevertheless, Portnoy assured me that Mrs. B's mistrust and tendency to accuse me would be "worked out."

That proved to be wishful thinking. By the end of December Mike and I were back in Bradshaw House.

Portnoy called us and our father into the office for "a mutual discussion". He asked us where we would like to go if we had a choice. We were "very glib" and "denied [our] feelings." It was "up to you," we said. Portnoy made the situation clear: We could stay only a few days at Bradshaw House. We could not go home to our father, for we needed more supervision than he could provide. Maybe the agency could find a foster home in another town, but probably not close enough to Solomon Lewenberg for us to continue studying there. That was the only option.

Our experience of a foster home had lasted just short of three months. At its conclusion Portnoy remarked in his report: "Important: All the feelings toward food and foster mother are related to boys' feelings toward own mother, which they were not able to work through."

How right he was.

Had the agency succeeded in helping Mike and me "work through" our feelings toward our mother, it surely would have encountered the root of my resentment of my foster mother: my unwillingness to accept the loss of my mother and my anger that another woman should presume to take her place. Here I speak only for myself. Mike and I never discussed feelings. But in the absence of agency-sponsored psychological analysis I offer two sets of circumstances that make the reason for my intransigence clear: my need to attend Solomon Lewenberg Junior High School and my attempt to keep my green flannel shirt.

What no one, including myself, understood about my dedication to the school was the fact that my mother had played a role in my attending it. She had been home from the hospital for several months, seemingly well enough to contemplate the possibility that Mike and I might stay over on some weekends if her doctor approved. It was early September and time to register for the imminent academic year at a school new to us both, for Mike was entering junior high school for the first time, and my prior school in Roxbury no longer served as a junior high school.

Together, my mother, Mike, and I boarded the orange streetcar and set out. Together, we traveled by Franklin Park, made the right turn onto Blue Hill Avenue, and continued on to Mattapan. I silently cherished what I imagined strangers saw when they looked at us: just another mother and her sons rather than separate pieces of a very troubled family.

We climbed the big hill, entered the school, and walked through the hall toward the murmuring gymnasium where scores of kids stood at tables, doing the necessary paper work. There were few parents present but I wasn't embarrassed by my own. This was my mother, who had insisted to Mr. Portnoy that she accompany us despite the fact that it was his job and despite feeling unwell. This was my mother, who was proud of us, and cared that we enroll in a school she considered superior to the one designated for us by the Boston School Committee. She stood beside us and, smiling brightly, talked to the seated woman behind the table while we filled out the forms. We sat together during the principal's address in the auditorium and, riding home, we talked excitedly about the grand prospects that stretched before us at "Solly".

In less than three months my mother was dead. I was not going to let go of that school any sooner than I had to.

Nor would I part with my ragged flannel shirt, a present from my mother two or three years before. It was mostly green with red and white, a kind of faded plaid. It was much too small for me to wear and very soft, like an oft-laundered baby's blanket. It lacked several buttons—opalescent they had been—and those that remained were useless, for the buttonholes were stretched beyond any capacity to contain them. Elbows, cuffs and collar were torn or frayed and whitened at the edges. In short, it bore little resemblance to a shirt and was good for nothing but to be a rag, and a poor one at that. I did not try to use it as a shirt. It lived quietly behind the other clothes in my bureau drawer. I did not need to see it or touch it or smell it to know that it was there.

When the blonde lady who would become my new foster mother said we should throw it away, that it had served me and that it was time to part with it, I said no, I liked it and wanted to keep it. We were sitting on the bedroom floor with a pile of clothes and she looked at me curiously and then she said o.k., if that's what you want, and continued in silence to help me put my clothes away. I was careful to fold my shirt the way my mother had taught me to fold a shirt and I put it behind everything, in the left rear corner of the drawer. Several months later I discovered that it was gone. I never mentioned its disappearance, nor my feeling of betrayal, not to anyone, but today I can imagine that it was painful for my foster mother to have such a thing in her house despite my attachment to it.

Within two weeks of Mike's and my leaving the B's home the agency found and approved another foster family for us. Mr. and Mrs. E. lived with their three children in Winthrop. The care with which Portnoy managed this placement indicates not only what he had learned in the past several months about the complexity of the transition process but how much was riding on the Winthrop home's success. He made two preliminary visits, once with his supervisor, and concluded that Mrs. E. seemed a "much more relaxed" woman than Mrs. B., willing to allow us the freedom we needed. We were to feel that this was our home and that we could eat as much as we wanted.

Portnoy brought Mike and me for a preliminary visit and left us there for dinner and conversation with Mrs. E. "The boys were happy that we found them a home," he reported later. In his final case notes before leaving the agency as a Fulbright Scholar, he was able to say that Mike and I seemed to feel like family members, that "there was a real togetherness in this family unit," that the boys had found a "wonderful" home.

And it was only an hour by bus, train and streetcar to Solomon Lewenberg!

Portnoy's replacement, Paul Dubroff, also observed that Mike and I were "doing very well," making "an excellent adjustment." Although our foster mother characterized that adjustment as "wonderful in every respect," she wanted Dubroff to know that when Mike and I had first come we were often "sullen and resentful, unwilling to address her directly." Only after "considerable work" on her part, she said, were we able to relax. Now, it seemed, we regarded the E. home as our own.

It seemed, too, that Mike and I were coming to terms with having a foster mother without resenting her for her displacement of our natural mother. Once, Mrs. E. told Dubroff, "Benjy took out a picture of his mother which he kept in his wallet because he wanted Mrs. E. to see this." And often, when she had cooked a particular dish and brought it to the table, "Mikey and Benjy would smile and say 'This is just how my mother used to make it.'"

What accounted for this change?

My father's attitude, for one. His hostility toward the idea of a foster home placement had clearly contributed to our rejection of the Bs, but he felt very comfortable with our new foster family. Mrs. E. noticed how much happier he seemed since his boys were doing so well. Initially, she told Portnoy, before a visiting regimen was established, he would come every Sunday and sit with the family. Later, when once a month he came to visit Mike and me, she invited him to dinner. On the remaining Sundays we visited him in Roxbury. There he praised our foster parents whom, he felt, sincerely cared for us. "It is evident," Dubroff recorded, "that he feels in a way a part of the E. family and looks forward to his Sunday visits."

Also, the family dynamics were different. Mrs. B. "was very rigid," Portnoy noted in his summary report, meant to introduce his successor to our case. She "could not understand these adolescent boys' needs. She was suspicious of them and the boys were very unhappy there." They needed more "maternal understanding" than she could provide them. Mrs. E., on the other hand, currently had two early adolescent girls of her own, and a more relaxed personality than Mrs. B. She was in touch with the freedom we required and that made for a relaxed relationship unpolluted by suspicion.

Other circumstances, too, were decidedly different. Our father had finally sat down with Mike and me and told us that living with him in the near future was not an option. He had come to believe that we needed "a few more years' care" before returning to Roxbury, that supervision was essential if we were to avoid getting into "some difficulty" with the wrong sort of people. We had learned, too, that we had outgrown Bradshaw House, that the agency would tolerate only a short stay there while it found another foster home for us. There was no going back. A foster home was the only feasible solution to the problem of what to do with us and we were smart enough to know that we had better come around to that position.

Then there is the possibility that things were not as rosy in the E. home as they seemed, that early on everyone made a sincere effort to get along as one happy family, but eventually that effort—and again I speak only for myself—failed. For despite the caseworkers' observations I rarely felt that I was a full member of my foster family. Certainly I never felt that my foster parents loved me (and looking at the situation from their perspective, I suppose I wasn't particularly loveable). Mike lived with the E.,s for several years, right up to the day he married. Although we never spoke of the matter, he seemed to me untroubled by my concerns. I felt that he was much more attuned to the family's dynamics and culture than I who, as I grew older, wanted only to distance myself from my foster home, spending a large amount of time with the family of my friend, Howard Rosenberg.

Now a professor of art at the University of Nevada at Reno, Howard recently reminded me during a rare visit to Manhattan of the distance he perceived fifty years ago between me and my foster parents. He was richly enjoying his corned beef on rye sandwich at the Carnegie Deli when he paused and said, "Benj, I knew where you lived, but I was never in the house. You never introduced me to your foster family, and never showed any interest in doing so. Your life with the Es was totally separate from our life together." Licking his lips, Howard continued, recalling his mother's words: "I don't think Benji is very happy. We need to be sure that he knows that he and Michael can come here as long as they want and as often as they want." Mike never took advantage of this open invitation; Howard was not his friend and, indeed, he never felt the need. But I found a second home with the Rosenbergs.

It was Howard's mother, Rosalie, who took me during the fall of my freshman year to Filene's basement to buy a winter coat. She told me as we drove through the tunnel into Boston that she did so as much for my mother's sake as for mine. She spoke of her friendship with my mother years before when they had both lived in Roxbury and said my mother was "the sweetest woman in the world." I am sure that the personal connection between Rosalie Rosenberg and my mother largely explains why I felt a level of family comfort with the Rosenbergs that I seldom felt in my foster home.

I want to make it clear that I consider myself fortunate to have lived in the E. home. As my foster sister, Sharon, said in a letter she wrote to me, they were "giving people" who wanted to shelter children who needed a good home. Sharon misses the mark by almost a century when she asserts that foster homes were "non-existent" in 1955, when Mike and I came to Winthrop, and proudly praises her parents for being on the "cutting edge" of this practice, but more important than strict accuracy here is her overall memory of a salutary family life.

She "can't remember" a meal without home made food aplenty: "pot roast with real mashed potatoes not instant . . . roast chicken with roasted potatoes . . . and her soups and borchts were all home made . . . lentil soup, chicken soup, matzo ball soup . . . She made home made desserts too . . . mandelbread, strudel, coffee cakes and we always had birthday cakes." The way she remembers it, she and her mother wore hand-me-down clothes while Mike and I had new clothes bought with the money given her parents by the agency—a new jacket every fall. The "little money" from the agency was "never enough, but they made it stretch . . . They weren't into it for the money."

While I believe that Sharon's memories of her family's life during those years are rather sanguine, I agree with her essential contention that her parents provided all their children, natural and foster, with a home that amply satisfied their physical needs. Nor do I wish to take issue with her arguably exaggerated memories regarding her parents' awareness of our and our foster sisters' and brother's emotional needs.

"My parents," she writes, "had to meet with the case worker almost every month, and I had to as well to make sure we were happy with things. The whole family was being scrutinized to make sure everything was what it seemed to be. If any of us were unhappy or had a problem it had to be discussed with the caseworker, Mr. Dubroff. I would come home from school and he and my mom would be sitting at the kitchen table over coffee and cake discussing the family. Nothing was personal. He knew everything, but that was his job. He had to know how you and Mike were doing as well as how Jeff, Vivian and I were doing. We were considered a family."

It's just that *I* rarely felt that way.

I wanted to feel closeness to my foster mother, wanted things to work out, and attempted to ignore my feelings of alienation from her and to convince myself that there was no real problem in the relationship. To the world I maintained an untroubled demeanor. But I suppose I have always resented the peculiar strain of emotional neglect that gradually developed in the years I spent with the Es and that eventually could not be ignored. Today, equipped with a larger perspective than the one I possessed as a child, I can see that I wanted what I could not have: a foster mother who could replace my own mother or, more precisely, a foster mother whose love could replace my fantasy of my mother's love.

When the time came I chose to attend the University of Massachusetts, in the western part of the state, although I had been accepted bytwo universities in Boston to which I could have commuted. But I wanted to be away from what I deemed to be Winthrop's parochial environment, and I wanted to establish a physical distance between me and my foster family, a parallel to the emotional distance that lay between us. By that time Dubroff and I had agreed that my attendance at a school far from Winthrop "would add much" to my growth.

Even much later, when I had married, had children, and bought a house, my invitation to them to come visit was met with silence. On the infrequent occasions when we do see each other, such as at funerals, my foster mother will vocally regret the distance between us, the loss over the years of the inclusive family, but the prospect of more sympathetic relations has never gone beyond words. I readily admit that I have not worked to make those words a reality.

My case file has allowed me to understand what happened between me and my foster mother over the three and a half years that I lived with her in Winthrop, before I lived mostly away, at college. During the initial stage of our relationship, I am sure, I agreed with Portnoy that she "really is an extremely warm person and a very giving, understanding woman." And I am sure that Mike and I "became very fond of her and also with [my foster father] and the three children."

Portnoy was "always impressed" with her ability to give equally of herself to her children as well as to Mike and me. He left the agency before that perception could be tested by time, but he did follow up his positive observations with a "however," the substance of which eventually rendered me unable to consider myself a true member of the family.

Portnoy's "however" continued: "now and then she would make requests [for] more money." She had remarked to Portnoy that Mike and I had "tremendous appetites" and freedom to go to the fridge with her permission. Consequently, she thought that the agreed-upon sum of $60. per month board rate for the two of us should be raised to $70. Portnoy presented the request to the agency and "in view of the excellent adjustment the boys were making" the rate was raised to $70, although the initial amount was to have covered such exigencies as our growing boy appetites.

The increased funding came with conditions. Mrs. E. was expected to launder our shirts herself and take care of incidentals we might need. (The agency would continue to provide allowances and carfare). She was also expected to submit receipts for the money she had laid out in order to be compensated for her expenditures for medicines, shoe repair, cleaning and "like items."

Several months later Dubroff discussed the "board payment situation" with Mrs. E., who had submitted, without receipts, a number of expense items including ironing of shirts, milk money and a large sum for medicines. She was "made aware" by Dubroff that the rate had been increased to cover precisely this kind of expense, that milk as food could not be considered a separate expense, and that their agreement required receipts if compensation for her expenses was to be made.

Awareness that a foster home relationship with the agency was partially a financial arrangement came early to me in Winthrop. I was a bright boy and had always enjoyed listening to adult conversation, as my housefathers did not fail to observe. But that awareness did not trouble me. Rather, it was the fallout from my foster mother's financial quarrel with the agency that did. Here is an excerpt from Dubroff's report regarding the "very long talk" he had with Mrs. E:

> She reacted with considerable hostility, was most controlling and made very thinly disguised threats of terminating the placement should the agency not accept her demands . . . [She] became quite negative, claiming that she knew that the non-Jewish agencies not only paid a larger board rate but were much more liberal with expenses and that she wondered if the agency really had the welfare of the children in mind when they argued over what seemed to be such small sums . . . and suggests not too indirectly that she feels that she would consider giving up the children as much as she likes them. She felt the need to tell worker that she certainly is not motivated through profit.

Dubroff's supervisor explained to him that the agency would accede to Mrs. E.'s demands "in view of [her] hostility which might have threatened the placement or have spread to the boys."

This situation developed at the end of Mike's and my first year in Winthrop. Its substance must have clouded the previously sunny relationship between the agency and our foster mother. I contend that the knowledge of her willingness, if thwarted, to give us up did, indeed, "spread to the boys" and gradually soured the promising relationship between Mrs. E. and me. And as if to confirm the incipient feeling of alienation I must have brooded over, another incident of the same tenor developed.

Two months after the blowup of peaceful relations between the agency and Mrs. E. I learned that Mike and I were to leave the Winthrop home for the summer. Mrs. E. had "announced," Dubroff recorded, that she and her husband and children were going to California for a vacation. She wanted the agency to remove us from her home and she wanted the agency to pay her a retainer fee. Later the trip was canceled and the family planned to remain in Winthrop, "but [she] still wanted the boys out for the summer." Mike and I would go to Bradshaw House and to camp.

In his office, Dubroff asked me what I felt about the summer and the Es' plans. I had little to say about my feelings. I simply "guessed" Mike and I would go to Bradshaw House. Dubroff wrote: "Indeed there seemed to be less feeling against this plan than one would have expected."

Dubroff's impression of my response to his question was that I was a "rather passive adolescent." This was doubtlessly true, but had he known me longer he would have understood, because of my history with the agency and the conclusions of psychological examinations, that I was prone to bury my negative feelings deep and attempted to maintain an untroubled façade in order to avoid intrusions into my emotional life. While my actual response to the ease with which the Es were willing to dismiss me and Mike was anger, I projected a calm surface and quietly, privately, withdrew from involvement with my foster family.

During the semester break of my junior year at UMass events seemed to me to confirm my feelings of alienation from my foster parents. I returned to Winthrop to learn that I could room and board with them no later than the start of the next academic year. They wanted their youngest child to have his own room. They had also taken in Henry, another boy from the agency, displacing me from my bed. Shortly afterward, as my new caseworker, Herman Steingraph, and I were winding up our interview, I off-handedly told him the Es were "tossing me out." My foster father had broken the news to me "in a kind of joking way." Steingraph observed that I seemed "hurt" by my foster parents' decision and I—even I—agreed. Despite that expression of anger, I admitted to some ambivalence regarding my feelings toward my foster family.

But I felt no ambivalence regarding my living arrangements. I was determined to make my own. I intended to take the Rosenbergs up on their offer. I told Steingraph that Mrs. E. was opposed to this plan, that she did not want me living in Winthrop "because it would reflect badly on her own children." When Steingraph spoke to her he concluded "that she was very much aware of the prospective home for B. being also in Winthrop and this might reflect upon her as the good foster mother." Another foster family in another town, she suggested, or the "Y" in Boston, would be best for me.

I preferred the "Y" any day to another foster home, I told Steingraph, but insisted on living with the Rosenbergs. Steingraph agreed that I was "a sufficiently responsible youngster to make [my] own . . . arrangements."

Which I did.

"The Couch"

Nancy Linder Nancy Linder Nancy Linder

I couldn't stop thinking about Nancy Linder. Her name was a mantra, a mantra whirling its way throughout my mind, my whole being, but especially throughout my groin, carried there by my pulsing blood until nothing existed but Nancy Linder and it.

It was my seventh summer in Winthrop. I knew I had outgrown the place. I had lived for six years as a foster child with my foster parents and their three children and my brother. I had graduated after three years of Winthrop High School, had completed three years at UMass, and was impatiently awaiting my senior year in Amherst before leaving for good.

We met at the beach. She was sitting on a dark green towel, leaning against the concrete sea-wall. The straps of her bright red bathing suit had fallen from her tanned shoulders. Her lips were slightly open as Herb made the introductions. I could see the tips of her white teeth. They glistened.

Herb and I were friends from UMass. He had been driving when Mary Capuchin jumped all over me in the back seat of his Chevy. I could see his face in the rear view mirror. His eyes grew large. That incident had earned me an extra degree of respect from

Herb. His own date was Nancy's cousin, as it turned out, and Nancy was currently a guest for the summer at her cousin's beach house. With this information imparted I breathed a silent sigh. Summer's prospects had certainly changed for the better.

I had been standing while Herb introduced me, smiling down at Nancy Linder. The vantage point was excellent and I hesitated to leave it, to bend my knees and lower myself to the sand beside her. I was enjoying the faint suggestion of her cleavage and the roundness of her breasts edging up to the top of her suit and I didn't want to stop. My glasses were fogging up and I wasn't sure it was all due to the heavy air on the beach. Suddenly I became aware of prickling sensations in my genitals and sat down quickly to conceal any evidence of what I was so obviously experiencing. And I knew by her eyes and the way she adjusted her red straps that she knew at least some of what I was feeling and encouraged it.

We talked, the four of us, and then I proposed to Nancy that we walk along the tide line and let the water lap about our toes. She nodded and I stood and extended my hand to her and she grasped it and I pulled and she squealed and, standing and still holding my hand, remarked that my bright blue bathing suit went well with hers. And we were off.

Two weeks later, Vivian, the eldest of the E. children, reported to her mother that she had seen me lying with a girl on a blanket at the beach, embracing and kissing. That was cause enough for my foster mother to lecture me that evening on beach propriety. "Benjie," she said, confronting me in the knotty pine kitchen alcove where I had eaten my first meal in the house and done so much of my homework through high school. "Benjie, those things are not for public display. They are for private times. Control yourself, dear. Be a *mensch*."

She was right. I knew it then as well as I know it now. (I cannot say with any trace of truth that I knew it while embracing and kissing

Nancy Linder). But I was not about to be a *mensch* on my foster mother's terms.

There were times, I admit, when I felt quite comfortable in the E. midst. The pear tree out back yielded good eating fruit and picking them with a long pole and a metal basket on the end was an art I recall being taught by my foster father. There was the warm summer evening, the air suffused with brine, when we all rode to the boardwalk at Revere Beach. The hot oven pizza we shared burnt the tops of our mouths almost simultaneously. There was the tale and the smiles it provoked of dancing in the aisle to the beat of Benny Goodman's orchestra. Certainly there were times like these, but often I felt like a stranger.

I was a reader and there were few books in the house. I enjoyed the poetry of Frost and cummings and read all of Steinbeck and much more and was admired by everyone as a kind of intellectual freak. My brother loved basketball and his ability in the sport drew ardent, unqualified admiration from the whole family. That was just fine with me as long as I was left undisturbed to read my books.

And then there was the new couch.

It was encased in a greenish gold plush and dominated the living room, positioned as it was against the raised tan and cream wood of the patterned wall behind it. To anyone who entered the room it commanded, in couch talk, a language I clearly understood: "Do not sit on me. I am here to be admired only. That is why there is a clear plastic cover all about me. Do not even think of sitting down on me. I am not to be enjoyed. I am to be displayed. Go away."

Mrs. E. had advised me one day to marry a girl with money, and I knew she meant what she said. If to be a *mensch* was to have money and own a couch like this, I wanted none of it. If to be an admirable person, a man with fine character, was to live in a house without books and poetry, and with a couch that threatened me with death by absolute airlessness, breath prohibited by plastic, being a *mensch* was not for me.

And in case you were wondering, that is why I require these moments of your time to tell you of my summer romance with Nancy Linder. It was she who would be my unwitting accomplice in rejecting the couch's commands and all that they represented.

It was an August evening, almost the end of the school vacation, and they were all away at a basketball tournament. The house was still. The smiling host, I ushered Nancy through the front door and through the sun porch and into the living room. We were face to face with the presence of the couch. Its plastic covering glowed in the evening light stealing into the room. We were there to embrace and kiss, but this time in private, just as Mrs. E. preferred.

Exchanging guilty glances, the two of us carefully removed the couch's plastic shroud, Nancy on one end and I on the other, each of us remembering how to replace it when we had concluded our tryst. It lay limp and powerless piled there in the middle of the room while Nancy and I enjoyed ourselves. Perhaps it was an hour we spent there, perhaps more, perhaps less. Time was of no consequence. Nancy's mouth was warm and soft and sweet. She smelled like lilacs and her hands were eager and her breasts were round.

When we were done with our embracing and kissing we carefully smoothed the plush fabric and re-covered the couch with its plastic, now so ludicrously vulnerable. Holding hands, we walked to Nancy's cousin's house in the breeze-freshened air and failing light. I felt no pride in what we had done but I felt good about it anyway.

It wasn't the last time I would see Nancy Linder, but almost. Soon I would leave for my final undergraduate year and then the world would be mine to make of it what I could.

Case Studies

My own experience, then, is not the stuff of a convincing argument that in the absence of a viable natural-family life only a foster home can provide the individual attention and love a child requires. Indeed, I am surprised by the degree of bitterness I still feel regarding my foster home experience. In any case, I know that I was never the grade of "foster home material" the agency perceived me to be. I believe, again, that the agency's unblinking commitment to foster home placement as the ultimate goal of its casework policy obscured the fact that some children would never be as happy in foster homes as they were in group homes.

That commitment, as discussed by Barbara Miller Solomon in *Pioneers In Service*, was the product of an ideological conflict that reached back more than a century. Despite extensive and promising experimentation with foster care and the strongly voiced opinions of officials and workers in charitable agencies that outmoded orphanages were inferior to foster home care, many in control—and in particular the Ladies Helping Hand Auxiliary—remained "committed to their belief that dependent children could best be served under one institutional roof." In 1933, however, the Federation of Jewish Charities endorsed widespread foster home placement. Three years later, led by its new director, Dora Margolis, the federation expanded its professional casework programs, and within a decade there was no question that those who had championed casework professionalism and foster home placement in charitable childcare had triumphed. As if to certify that result, in 1946 the Ladies Helping Hand Home for Jewish Children, a thirty-two room Greek revival mansion in Brighton, fell under the administrative control of the newly organized Jewish Family and Children's Service of Boston. There distressed children would be studied and counseled until they could return to their families or be placed in foster homes.

It was within this historical context that I, Mike, and scores of other children who needed a home other than our own for some period of time found ourselves under the supervision of the Jewish Family and Children's Service of Boston. While we knew little of the agency forces dedicated to steering us from group homes toward foster homes when judged to be "foster home material", there was no escaping them. That is to say, there was no escaping Beatrice Carter.

Margolis recruited Carter from Smith College where she had served as a lecturer, a supervisor of student caseworkers, and finally as the field representative of Smith's School of Social Work. Until her retirement in 1953 she worked closely with Margolis to shape the agency's program. She brought her considerable strengths and puzzling weaknesses to her positions as Caseworker Consultant, Assistant Director for Administration and Casework, and finally Director of Children's Service. From that unassailable position she profoundly affected the lives of many children and adolescents.

Carter's earlier professional correspondence with her superior, Dr. Everett Kimball, Director of the Smith School of Social Work, reveals her incisive, unyielding, yet compassionate character as she evaluated the abilities of student caseworkers and their supervisors:

In a letter to Kimball (April 27, 1940) Carter reports that she has removed Harriet D. from the field because "she seemed absolutely unable to grasp the responsibilities which her position as a social worker would have required of her."

Carter wrote (Oct. 10, 1939) of a student about whom Kimball had expressed reservations, and included an evaluation of her supervisor:

> Mrs. K. is a most desirable supervisor for second year students. Early in contact she sensed Miss S.'s insecurity in relation to people. She worked with her persistently and thoughtfully (and so did I), in order to lead her to painless termination of her training. Miss S., despite her personal charms, which will probably make her happy in her life as a wife, proved to be entirely incapable of learning. She plans to go into the field of public relief, in which case we may be able to modify our expectations of her, letting her go her own pace and graduating with the full knowledge that she will not produce on any job the same results that we expect of others.

In the same letter Carter reports that M.'s supervisor and she

> were dubious about Miss M.'s potentialities as a caseworker. She showed very little psychological insight, meeting all problems of work and supervision with a rather shallow approach. She had to be forced to do some profound thinking. I mention this student only because of the unusual change that occurred to her since her coming to training. Thanks to the work of the supervisor, Miss M. is nowhere as anxious as she was during her last few days at Smith and first few weeks in Philadelphia. She appears to be a brilliant, capable girl.

Carter's judgments suggest the terror her intense character must have engendered in some of her students, but also her compassionate nature:

> She seems so very anxious. When she first came into the room for conference with me, she bent almost double in what appeared to be anxious expectation of something drastic . . . When you see her, deal with her easily and gently as I know you are apt to. It may be that the best service we can do for her would be after trying it for a little while, tell her that casework is not the field where she will function with the greatest of ease.

These representative excerpts regarding Carter's dealings with the adults she supervised, taken from letters housed in the Smith College Archives in Northampton, Massachusetts, must cause us to acknowledge the effect her relentless pursuit of high professional standards had upon agency policy. Certainly they reveal her to have been fully capable of absolute commitment to a standard she believed in and consequently incapable of appreciating the relative virtues of an opposing standard. Nevertheless, consideration of the experiences of several agency wards may allow us to understand that the more "progressive" strategy of foster home placement was not for everyone:

None of the following three agency wards with whom Mike and I lived in Brighton and Dorchester was ever placed by the agency in a foster family. All returned to their parents. However, their memories reveal the considerable merits of the agency's group home management.

DANNY

Danny was my friend in Bradshaw House. His expression is serious as he sits near me in my photograph of the Solomon Lewenberg

Junior High School graduating class of 1955. His greeting is on the back: "To a Bradshaw House Bum from Another". I had seen Danny only once in the fifty years since that spring when the photograph was taken. He was that noisy teenager who ranged up and down the Fenway bleacher steps shouting "Peanuts! Peanuts!!" We talked briefly but he had no time for conversation. As it turned out Danny became a "top vendor" and his success selling peanuts led to his operating a souvenir concession in Fenway Park for thirty-two years. He worked during the off-season as a waiter and a purchasing agent for a chemicals company. He and his wife, Lynda, raised three children. Indebted to the Hebrew Immigrant Aid Society's expertise at finding people, I met Danny again at his daughter's family condo north of Boston.

Danny and I had much in common beyond Solomon Lewenberg and Bradshaw House. Our homes were within walking distance of each other (Danny lived on Blue Hill Ave). His mother was dying of stomach cancer during the more than two years he lived in Bradshaw House. His father, an addicted gambler, worked at two jobs and could not care for his four children. None of Danny's five aunts was willing to take in him or his two sisters. We celebrated our bar mitzvahs within weeks of each other and at the same temple. But Danny lived at Bradshaw House much longer than I and eventually moved to the home of his father and new stepmother.

Despite a recent stroke, Danny was exuberant when I asked him about his memories of Bradshaw House. He remembered everything and spoke of it all with delight: stories about the kids and the housefathers; shouting "My seat coming back!" to reserve a choice place by the TV; roller skating at the Chez Vous; dance parties with girls from the Brighton home; trips to the Brookline High School swimming pool and to the paddle boats of Norumbega Park; and much more. He loved the freedom that allowed him to walk from Bradshaw House to his *bobi's* home in Roxbury, where she owned a candy store and cared for Danny's older brother. He talked with great affection for the place and for the people who made so much a joy to him, as if Bradshaw House had been a summer camp. "It wasn't like what you think of as a 'home,'" Danny said, glowing.

Remembering the fellowship of his peers and, as it seemed, being continually engaged in pleasurable activities, Danny sat on the couch with my tape recorder between us and sighed: "I just had a good time . . . I had a lot of fun at Bradshaw House." Danny's sister, Sylvia, added from across the room: "They were very good to us. I felt privileged, actually." I asked Danny if he felt the same way. His reply was an immediate and emphatic "Yes".

SYLVIA

During the two years and two months Danny lived in Bradshaw House, Sylvia lived with her older sister, Claire, in the study home. They were among my housemates, although I retain little memory of them. Like Danny, Sylvia talked in superlatives when discussing her experience with the agency, but was more forthcoming than Danny when the discussion turned to emotional needs. For instance, although Danny shared with me the fact of his bedwetting and admitted that the Bradshaw boys often teased him about it, he made light of what must have been a painful situation, insisting that the consequences of his enuresis amounted to nothing and passing them off as part of "growing up". Hearing this, Sylvia pithily remarked: "If anyone needed mental health in those days, it was us."

Sylvia praised the home's staff for their response to her emotional needs. For six months they disregarded the home's policy of determining the children's sleeping arrangements by age, understanding that the sisters needed to be together and in a room separate from the others. She remembered Rorschach tests "every five or six months," conversations with her caseworker, and forced rest periods after meals to counter her serious hyperactivity. Most affectionately, she gleefully recounted the story of stealing into the room where the Chanukah presents were kept, if only to admire the brightly wrapped packages, and being let off for her transgression with a brief lecture without anger or meanness.

"They gave us so many wonderful gifts," Sylvia remembered, and the tone of her voice indicated that those gifts were not limited to the material. Starved for love at home due to a mother too sick to care for her and a father who favored his sons while ignoring his daughters, she found love in Brighton. "It wasn't a large amount of kids; it was sort of intimate," she recalled. "I cried because I didn't want to go in there and I cried because I didn't want to leave . . . It was a wonderful place." Her voice grew soft when she summed up her response to the time she lived in Brighton: "I have warm, wonderful feelings about the home. I felt a lot of love there, you know."

As for the material gifts, Sylvia credits "the rich side of the family" for arranging her and Claire's residence in the study home. "You had to have a connection to get in there," she believes. "It wasn't a welfare place. It was the best of everything." She particularly enjoyed the gift of summer camp in Maine and the new bicycles the children pedaled up and down the long drive to and from the big, white house. There, whether material or immaterial, so much was offered her that would not have been possible at home.

"It was two years of my life that I wish had continued," Sylvia sighed, but she would have given up everything to be living with a healthy mother in a happy family. She prayed for that, rearranging her life every evening before going to sleep, fantasizing that her mother had become well and that she and Claire would soon return to their home in Dorchester.

Only the return to her home was to be. Her mother died and when Sylvia was ten her father remarried and withdrew his children from the agency's custody. The girls returned to a family life barren of love—to a father whose relationship with his daughters Sylvia described as "emotionally brutal," and to a stepmother who felt only animosity toward them. Both parents physically beat their daughters. Sylvia perceived her stepmother as a "witch," a "stepmother from Hell" who intentionally said hurtful things to her and treated her and Claire as serfs, forcing them to do the housework while she filed and painted her nails. Eight years would pass before Sylvia, the last to do so, managed to break free of her parents. Until then, she said, "I was in hell." Remembered from such a distance, life in the study home must have seemed the faintest of lovely dreams.

BOB

Bob's brother, Meyer, "had it all" at home, and Bob deeply resented his dominance. Two years older, Meyer constantly picked on Bob and, when his parents were out of the apartment, beat him with a length of rubber hose, the thick, black kind you might find under the hood of your car. As Bob tells it, his father often beat him with the same hose as punishment for infractions reported by Bob's mother. She, however, constantly lied to protect her older son, leaving Bob to face the consequences: "whap, whap . . ." She was dead set against me," Bob said of his mother.

To illustrate the insidious family dynamic, Bob told me the story of how, one evening, Meyer beat his sick, brain-damaged sister. Having wrested the hose from his brother, Bob had it in his hand when his parents entered the apartment and found their daughter bruised and in tears. Following a familiar pattern, he was about to receive punishment for something he had not done when his sister pointed to Meyer and yelled: "He did it! He did it!"

Bob was never beaten for his chronic "hooking" of school, however. His mother wanted him to attend school, but his father was too tired when he returned home from work to care or to do anything about his son's behavior in this respect. Bob cites his dislike of crowds as the motive for his truancy. He claims that the typical class size in his school was forty-five pupils and recalls that even at Fenway Park he would sit in the bleachers, way up by the big clock, as far away from other fans as he could get. Nevertheless, there is good reason to infer that his aversion to school stemmed from his hatred of being told what to do, a service his parents and brother performed all too insistently.

Bob eventually revealed his family circumstances to an aunt who happened to know Edward Portnoy. The two met and concluded that Bob urgently required distance from his family. Presented with this opinion, his parents agreed to a separation. Bob would live in Bradshaw House from 1953, at fourteen, to 1956, when he returned to his parents. In those three years he never went home, although his parents lived within easy walking distance of Bradshaw House. "Why should I?" he asked. "There was nothing there for me but problems."

"I felt real good at Bradshaw House," Bob said of his life there. Judging from several anecdotes he shared with me, Portnoy and other staff members must have agreed upon his acute need for non-threatening, positive, individual attention, for that is what they gave him.

Portnoy and Bob "got along great" despite the fact that Portnoy considered Bob's truancy a serious problem and directly addressed it. The two "had a talk" and Bob agreed to try attending school near the agency's Boston office where Portnoy could be more available to him and his teachers. But the experiment was short-lived. Rather than sit in class Bob rode the trains, trolleys and streetcars of the MTA throughout the day. Although he constantly urged Bob to attend school, "Portnoy was great" because "he never yelled at me; he never forced me to go to school." One day, Bob was at Bradshaw House shooting baskets when he should have been in school. Portnoy came by, sat, and watched him play. Then he shot some hoops, himself.

"Me and Mike got along great," Bob said of his relationship with Mike Fay, the handyman at the study home and Bradshaw House. Bob liked to help Mike out. Together they erected a backboard and hoop in the back yard and constructed the tall wooden wall against which we boys played darts and handball. He kidded Mike about the warped wood he believed Mike to be using and laughed at Mike's Irish brogue that "got me every time." Mike would finally respond, gruffly, "What are you laughing at?" and the two would laugh together. Sometimes they drove to Brighton and ate lunch with the girls.

Jules "Babe" Yosselivitz was captain of the Brandeis basketball team. He was also a housefather at Bradshaw House. Bob fondly remembers Babe's taking him to team practices and to several games: "Just me!" Once, back with Babe at Bradshaw House, Bob savored what he took to be a look of envy on Gerry Schlesinger's face, and for good reason.

"Gerry reminded me of my older brother," Bob said. He was "a wise guy" who "thought he was the boss," an intimidating presence to be avoided, never to be befriended. As far as Bob was concerned, everything had been perfect at Bradshaw House "until they brought Schlesinger in." Consequently, he deeply enjoyed the time a housefather put Gerry in his place. "You are not the boss here," he yelled. "Get up to your room and stay there!" And Gerry did. This was an achievement Bob could only dream of realizing with Meyer. No wonder he told the story with such exuberance.

It was important to Bob that his housefathers like him and that he like them. He thought they were "great," good company whether camping in New Hampshire with the Brighton girls or playing softball. He especially enjoyed the drive in 1954 to New York City through hurricane Carol with six kids and two housefathers in the car: the excitement of sharing an adventure, everyone together, trying to see the road. When I asked him if he thought his pleasure in these things was partially explained by others' caring for him he responded, slowly, as if considering the matter for the first time: "That might be, that might be." But there was no question that he valued his time at Bradshaw House as "excellent . . . I enjoyed everything we did."

Bob stoically accepted his return to his parents. He was seventeen and by agency standards too old to live with the younger boys. "I didn't like it too much but I guess it was my time to leave. I didn't say anything." Fifty years later, quietly speaking to me on the phone, Bob said it was "too bad I couldn't stay longer. I might have gone to school."

Bob moved with his family to a Boston suburb where his domestic difficulties resumed. He soon joined the Coast Guard but was discharged after three months for his failure to follow orders. Afterward he "wandered around," finding "a job here, a job there," and lived by his manual labor.

Given their accounts of life in Bradshaw House and the study home, I consider it unlikely that Danny, Sylvia, and Bob could have been better served in foster homes than they were in group homes. In their experience as in mine, life in the study home and Bradshaw House attained what was possible with regard to satisfying our physical and emotional needs. Their memories of that life are celebrations of the homes' management and regard for their welfare. Certainly foster home placement was the answer for many, such as my brother, but others did not fit the mold cast by the agency. Their psychological makeup would not permit it.

*   *   *

"Here," Len said, "keep it."

We hadn't seen each other in more than fifty years but he had just returned to the living room where we had talked for three hours and handed me a slender volume enclosed in a stiff, brown binder. The tattered label on the cover read: A Study of the Study Home of the Jewish Family and Children's Service of Boston February, 1946, to February, 1948 A Thesis Leonard Serkess B.U. S. of S.W. 1949. I could not have been more happily surprised to learn of this document's existence and to be able to use it for my own purpose.

Inside, as I later discovered, was an argument that championed two principles at the core of the agency's mission: commitment to foster home placement in the absence of the natural family, and reliance upon professional caseworkers to provide individual attention to parent and child. Len had submitted his dissertation only three years after the agency assumed control of the Brighton home. He meant to demonstrate the superiority of its principles to those of the prior, custodial, regime that provided no professional casework and considered the group home, itself, the end-all of residence until discharge.

To prepare the ground for his argument, Serkess studied the case files of forty-nine children who had lived in the study home for at least ninety days at some time between February, 1946, when the Ladies Helping Hand Auxiliary ceded its control of the home's administration, to February, 1948. Thirteen of these cases were children admitted before February, 1946; thirty-six were children admitted after that date. The ten cases Serkess selected to present "were indicative," he wrote, "of the type of situation handled at the Study Home and which best showed the application of the case work technique and use of the Study Home."

Frankly, I don't think he succeeded. In my opinion the ten case studies he presented do not offer enough information and analysis to support his argument. Nor did he develop his contention that the foster home was the "only" place, as he put it, a needy child can receive individual care and love.

But the effectiveness of a masters thesis written sixty years ago is unimportant to this memoir. Much more significant is the effect the ten case studies had on me. They brought front and center the overwhelming neediness of children whose circumstances cried out for the attention, kindness, and stability the agency sought to provide. Although these particular children lived in the study home at least two years before Mike and me and probably had all left before we came upon the scene in 1950, their cases involved issues with which we would become intimately familiar. This was not only their experience. It was also Mike's and mine.

As I read the case studies it dawned on me that each of the children knew some of the others, that most of the children knew—lived with—most of the others; that these ten children represented the very kind of community, though half as large, to which Mike and I would soon belong. We would bring to the same home (managed by Leonard Serkess!) our own troubled family background and our own symptoms of distress. We would be observed and helped by caseworkers and staff, psychologists and medical doctors, and evaluated to the end that we might be considered "foster home material," able to navigate the difficult transition from group home care to foster home placement. In sum, the case studies held up a mirror to me and urged me to accept a perspective I never had as a child and scarcely realized as an adult. It is in this context, rather than the one intended by Serkess, that I wish to present the circumstances of these children and the agency's response to them, whether or not they were bound for foster homes.

As a child, I did not think of Mike or myself as "needy" or "troubled," despite the anxiety for our welfare several adults in positions to know harbored without my awareness. I can recall only one occasion when I was fleetingly aware of the hard times a fellow ward had endured: seeing Gerry's mother as she painstakingly mounted the six wooden steps to the front door of Bradshaw House. Dashing from the dartboard in the back yard, I had just rounded the corner when I saw her. I noticed that her hair, pulled back severely on her head, was white and streaked with dark strands, and that her face was pale. She wore a frayed black coat and her back was bent and somehow I knew that *Gerry* (not his mother!) had it rough at home. I was a child and I thought as a child. Or, if I knew more than a child might be expected to know, I buried it deep and meant to keep it there.

As an adult, until recently, I wasn't any more analytical about these issues than I had been as a child. I did not think of myself or of the children with whom I lived as victims of family circumstances beyond our control. I simply did not think about these things, preferring to put them out of my mind. I suppose I just wanted that part of my past to go away. But the case studies considered here led me to acknowledge an experiential kinship with these children as well as a level of distress I had never admitted to others or to myself.

Although the accounts of their experiences as presented by Serkess are dated and rudimentary, they may explain the effect the case studies had on me. They may also shed some light on the issue of how best to administer much needed care.

Here are those accounts:

Stanley was eight when he entered the Ladies Helping Hand Home, a frightened child "oblivious to his surroundings." His mother had abandoned him and his father, who entrusted his own parents and then an orphanage with his son's welfare. These expedients failed, for Stanley was unable to trust anyone but his father and resorted to violent temper tantrums to ensure his presence. Because of his "limited intelligence" Stanley failed in school and the other children in the home ridiculed him. "He soon learned to develop his fighting ability and for a time he was uncontrollable and had practically all the children afraid of him." As he became more secure Stanley was less aggressive, but "was still unable to adjust away from his father, for whom he longed pathetically." After the agency gained responsibility for the home's management its psychologist diagnosed Stanley as "feeble-minded" and unlikely to adjust well there. The agency assigned him a caseworker who encouraged him to voice his needs and who counseled his father and grandparents to accept responsibility for his care. The agency released Stanley to his grandparents' custody after fourteen months in the home. There, Serkess concluded, he had "a good chance" of making an "adequate adjustment" to his world.

Murray was abandoned by both parents. His mother wanted no contact with him and moved to another state. His father showed no concern for his welfare. "A restless, aggressive boy," Murray whined and cried to get his way. Worse luck, "he was handicapped in his social adjustment by protruding teeth and a sinus condition which resulted in a running nose, which he rarely wiped." Despite the resources available to Murray nothing worked. He experienced several failures in agency foster homes prior to his arrival in Brighton in May, 1946. The agency psychiatrist, having evaluated Murray a second time, determined that he had positive feelings toward animals and Murray was accordingly placed in a farm family. But his inability to relate to others and his aggressive behavior led to another failed foster experience and he returned to Brighton. His caseworker hoped that the larger body of individuals there from which to choose friends might temper his aggression but nothing like that occurred, for Murray's deeply hostile presence served only to disturb the other children, who were younger than he and whom he bullied. Further evaluation suggested that Murray might do better among his peers and with more discipline. The agency sent him to the Bellfaire School in Cleveland, an institution that specialized in care for emotionally disturbed children. Murray ran away after three months. He had been so destructive that he was discharged *in absentia*. A plan to provide him with orthodontia came to nothing because of his instability. Serkess believed that only extensive psychotherapy "of the type that the Study Home was not equipped to offer" could have reached the source of Murray's anti-social behavior and allow him to accept proffered assistance. He eventually went to live with his mother upon her condition that he pay his own way.

Sylvia's mother died suddenly of a heart attack. Her father consigned her to four foster homes in the following year. All of these placements failed. At the end of that year, in February, 1948, ten-year-old Sylvia entered the study home. From the start she adjusted well to school and to life with the other children. The agency arranged for her to have piano lessons "which helped to keep her occupied and served as an outlet for some of her feelings." Despite these lessons Sylvia's caseworker believed the study home could offer her nothing "in the way of a true living situation, except care for her physical needs." Since she presented no serious emotional problems the agency believed she belonged in a foster home. But Sylvia's father required extensive casework before he could overcome his fear of losing his daughter to foster parents. Serkess wrote: "We have a situation here in which, were it not for the caseworker's preparation of the child for foster home placement and interpretation of this to the father, the child might very well remain in the Home for several years." Nevertheless, at the time Serkess submitted his thesis Sylvia was still living in the study home, still resisting, along with her father, foster home placement.

Shirley was three when her mother died of cancer. After unsuccessful attempts at living with relatives and with a psychologically troubled father whose attentions to her were "more physical . . . than is normal," she was admitted to the Ladies Helping Hand Home in 1944 and lived in Brighton for four and one-half years, more than two of those without benefit of a caseworker and without a program that identified and addressed her needs. "When she first entered . . . she was a quiet girl who presented few problems. Her main problem was enuresis, nocturnal and diurnal. She found it hard to relate to any one of the staff or children . . . She became very moody and her behavior was very unpredictable. She had crying spells that would leave her upset for hours, or even days, at a time." After the agency took charge its psychologist recommended that Shirley be placed in a home that "understood" her and where she would receive "firm guidance." She had been "institutionalized," Serkess wrote, by her lengthy residence in Brighton. Consequently, both she and her father found placement elsewhere difficult to accept. Extensive casework counseling, however, enabled them to do so. Placed in a farming family on the outskirts of Boston, Shirley was "adjusting excellently" when Serkess submitted his thesis.

Daniel's mother died giving birth to him at the Catholic Infant Asylum. He remained there for five and a half years, for his father was unable "to offer the boy any sort of stable home." Daniel was transferred to a Protestant home and then, in 1947, at age eight, to the study home, following a referral from the court, for in his short life he had amassed a lengthy record of lying and stealing. Daniel's relationship with the agency began at Camp Kingswood, the "casework camp" in Maine, where he was consistently hostile, fighting with and biting the other children. "Strictly a non-conformist," he built himself a little hut by the end of the camp session and remained in it as long as he could manage. At the study home in the fall he vigorously refused to wear shoes and to attend school. This behavior was reason enough to refer him to both a psychiatrist and a psychologist. They found him to be of average intelligence but unable to function normally because of "psychoneurotic conflict." The agency provided him with a private tutor and the home's staff paid special attention to his need to learn to live in a cooperative environment and to be accepted by a community. During this process Daniel recalled feeling the pain of being the only Jew in his former homes. At the study home he felt that he belonged. His caseworker maintained constant contact with his father and prepared him for Daniel's placement in a foster home five months after being admitted to the study home. There, Serkess remarked, "he would be able to receive individual care and love that only a foster home can offer."

Beverly was five when she was placed in the study home following her father's death and the onset of her mother's depression. She was small and undernourished, in the tenth percentile for both height and weight by the agency's development chart. "Her behavior was characterized by "negativism," whining and crying in order to get what she wanted. "She found it difficult to relate to people and was often by herself." The home's staff taught her to eat better and to become part of a group, to play games and to become more self-sufficient. After five months the agency placed her in a foster home in the country "so that she could have plenty of fresh air and sunshine," but only after she and her mother had been prepared by her caseworker to accept foster care."

Cynthia's parents were both "border-line psychotic individuals" who "had no sense of responsibility" for their child. After their divorce Cynthia's grandparents unsuccessfully assumed the burden of her care. Their attempts to place her in "nursery homes" failed and they turned her over to the Ladies Helping Hand Auxiliary in 1944 when she was four years old. When Cynthia entered the home she craved mothering. Often in tears, she found it hard to relate to others and generally made a poor adjustment. After the agency assumed responsibility for her care it assigned her a caseworker who found no personality problems and worked with the grandparents toward their accepting the child. After eighteen months Cynthia returned to their home.

Betty entered the study home in March, 1946. Her mother suffered from dramatic mood swings and her father showed little interest in his daughter. Both were contemplating divorce. They found several foster homes for Betty but all the placements failed because she "was unable to adjust without her parents," was unable to "accept any family unit other than her own." She adjusted well at the home and in school. When her parents decided to remain together she was discharged to them after only four months in Brighton.

Judy, admitted to the study home in July, 1946, was one of her mother's several illegitimate children. She had lived in a series of foster homes but all were unsuccessful because of her mother's constant interference; she was reluctant to give up her daughter despite being unwilling to keep her. Nothing is known of Judy's father. Because of her frequent moves from one foster home to another, some Jewish, others not, Judy became confused about her religious identity. She was also "unable to relate positively to people and found this very difficult." While Judy lived in the study home her mother married. This disturbed Judy and when her mother gave birth to another child she felt "entirely rejected." The agency provided psychiatric treatment for her and she learned from the home's staff to become part of a group and to live away from her mother. It was clear to the agency that Judy needed a foster home in which she could receive the individual attention she craved. It placed her in a foster home out of state after two years in Brighton. Serkess believed that casework with Judy's mother played a critical role in this situation. "It enabled her to accept the reality of her own position in regard to her ability to care for Judy and to further relinquish the child so that she would have an opportunity to develop to her fullest potentialities in a foster home."

Martin was seven when he entered the study home in 1947. Circumstances in his family had reached a crisis and neither parent was able to care for him. His mother, who had an extensive history of drug and alcohol abuse, was "deteriorating mentally." She was evaluated as a "mentally deficient person" and committed to the Boston State Hospital just before Martin's admission to the home. Martin's father was diagnosed with Parkinson's disease following encephalitis and was in no position to assume a parent's responsibilities. When their marriage began to fail each used

Martin as a pawn to spite the other and Martin, caught in the middle, became confused. This excerpt from his psychological evaluation, made shortly after his admission to the home, reveals his acute vulnerability:

> When Martin first entered the Study Home he was unable to help himself as well as some of the other children. This inability . . . plus his desperate need for protection and love caused him to seek out ways of 'buying' love. Whenever he received a package of food from home, he always gave most of it, if not all of it, away. Martin was very dependent upon his parents and eagerly looked forward to their visits.

Martin's parents placed him in the study home because they were unable to give him up directly to foster care or to relatives willing to care for him. The home's staff recognized Martin's over-generous nature and encouraged him "to win friends by making use of his personality and abilities." After months at the home he was able to complain if children hurt him, to stand up for himself, and to question staff decisions without fear of reprisal. He learned to dress himself, to act on his own behalf, to "develop his personality," and to be less dependent upon his parents. But Serkess argued that Martin's highly successful experience at the home was qualified by the likelihood of his becoming "institutionalized." By the time Serkess submitted his thesis a caseworker was working intensively with Martin and his parents so all could be comfortable with a foster home placement.

Nothing can be more disturbing to a child than the loss of his parents. Consequently, with the possible exceptions of Betty and Sylvia, these children were deeply troubled, for their parents were either dead or physically or psychologically unable to care for them. Whether the children's responses to their circumstances took the form of violence, or fear, or sorrow, or incapacity to interact, or any variation on these themes, they were indications of their neediness. The agency sought to understand those responses and to mitigate the children's pain with care and sensitive oversight by caseworkers and other agency personnel. In the long term it sought to address their neediness by foster home placement, a possible but problematic resolution that frequently required intensive casework with the children and their parents.

Mike and I shared these circumstances with the children presented in the Serkess thesis, and this fact brought home to me the understanding that in all likelihood we had been more troubled during our own childhoods than I ever realized or acknowledged.

But why was I so unprepared for this understanding? What was I thinking before I read Len's thesis, learned of these children's experiences, and felt enough of their pain to recognize it as my own? Obviously I had begun to think about this memoir before I knew of the thesis's existence. Did I not expect to become emotionally involved in the process of exploring our troubled childhoods? Did I not expect to encounter those troubles and our parents' and our own pain as never before? What was I doing—me, master of denial—turning up these long since buried artifacts if I wasn't prepared to discover unwelcome things?

I have often asked myself this question and I have concluded that I simply had not thought the process through, had subconsciously assumed I could continue to escape the painful awareness of the depth of our need. I would do my research into whatever documents or individuals turned up and write about the agency and its mission. I would express my gratitude to the many individuals who were there to help us. I would do this and escape unscathed once again. So I was unprepared for the details I encountered in our case files—the remarks about our mother's appearance and behavior, the observations of our father's inadequacy, and the evidence of our own vulnerability. I was unprepared for the emotions these details engendered in me. I felt like a smooth stone that had been defaced. I felt violated. I felt guilty for doing this to myself and to my mother and father and brother whose secrets, I told myself, I should have left undisturbed.

The social worker who handed me our case files had warned me that I would likely find material in them I might not wish to see. I listened to her and said "of course" but I didn't really hear. There was no need. I expected the armor I had always worn to protect me still. But my identification with the children in Len's thesis and, later, my absorption in the unearthed case files made it clear that it had not.

As to the propriety of foster home placement, Sylvia's and Betty's experiences reflect my opinion that while for some children, like Judy, foster homes can be the right strategy, for others they are not. Both failed to adjust to several foster homes. In Sylvia's case, her father was afraid of losing his daughter to other parents. Although Serkess does not specifically say so, Sylvia probably sensed her father's anxiety, as Mike and I did ours, and that induced a situation in which "she had to be removed" from her four foster homes, as we were from our first. As for Betty, Serkess clearly states that she "could not accept any family unit other than her own." Both girls adapted very well to the Brighton home after their foster placements failed. Sylvia and her father had not accommodated themselves to another placement by the time Serkess submitted his thesis. Betty was able to return to her parents.

I believe that children's expressions of satisfaction with extended group home life need not be perceived as the products of their unfortunate "institutionalization". Martin, for instance, had come a long way in defining his own character while living in the study home and he must have felt this and been proud of it. Although Serkess briefly credits the staff's sensitivity to his needs, his emphasis is elsewhere. He concludes by saying of Martin, "His over-acceptance of the Study Home situation indicates, of course, that if he remains at the Study Home too much longer, he will become institutionalized." Consequently, Martin and his parents were being prepared for foster home placement at the time Serkess submitted his thesis.

But in my opinion there is no "of course" to it. Martin's understandable pleasure in his changed living circumstances or Shirley's devotion to the study home need not be characterized as "over-acceptance" of a harmful condition. They might just as well be understood as testaments to the agency's enlightened group home management. As one who experienced almost four years of group home living, I prefer that interpretation. I cannot eat a blintz today without feeling a pang of loss for the nurturing I received at Bradshaw House.

New Americans

No one needed nurturing more than the children who had survived the Holocaust and traveled circuitous routes to become wards of Boston's Jewish Family and Children's Service. They had lost nearly everything: their parents and siblings, their homes, their communal lives—everything but their desire to move beyond their searing experiences.

As refugees after the war hundreds of children had endured months and years in Displaced Persons camps managed by the United Nations Relief and Rehabilitation Administration. They had been gathered up from there by organizations such as the American Committee for Orphaned Children and the Hebrew Immigrant Aid Society. These agencies entrusted them to welfare organizations, including chapters of the Jewish Family and Children's Service wherever that agency maintained a presence in the United States and Canada. Almost fifty of these children eventually found themselves in Boston. Like me and Mike and other Jewish-American survivors of broken homes, the new Americans were fortunate beneficiaries of the agency's concern and capacity to help them. But some of them, like some of us, were occasional objects of an institutional insensitivity toward their needs. That insensitivity was nourished by the agency's fiercely held beliefs that shaped its policies and were expressed, for better and for worse, by Beatrice Carter.

Having arrived in Boston with little advance notice, the first six or eight refugee children, entrusted to the agency by the European-Jewish Children's Aid, Inc., were brought to Camp Kingswood, in Bridgton, Maine. Supervised by Carter, who took up residence in a cabin there, they became oriented to their new circumstances and were psychologically evaluated by a psychiatrist and social workers. Afterwards, during the autumn of 1947, they began their new lives in America as residents of the study home, its Newton "annex", and Bradshaw House.

Several years after these children had grown and moved beyond the agency, the Child Welfare League, Inc., in the course of its evaluation of the services provided by the agency, went out of its way in its final report to commend the agency's care of its European wards:

> We would like to remark parenthetically on the splendid job that has been done with these children. The agency has given them exceptional care and enabled them to gain educational opportunities; to the outside observer it seems to have done its utmost to make certain that these homeless children have every opportunity to grow up to be full-fledged American citizens with the same rights and opportunities of native-born children. The total statistics on the questionnaires do not portray all the drama, thought and effort that have gone into these cases, but the fine work the agency has done in this area cannot be overestimated.

I have been able to contact and interview eight of the individuals who were refugee children aided by Boston's Jewish Family and Children's Service. Each warmly responded to my inquiries, whether in person while enjoying a meal or during telephone conversations. Three gave to me printed accounts of their experiences. The following pages in this chapter present what I have learned of their relationships to the agency and in particular to Carter.

I never met and never talked to Harry (Herszl) Singer, nor do I know what became of him. I found the following account in an agency commemorative publication edited by Ellen Fishman.

Harry was, at eleven, among the youngest of the children taken in by the agency. He had survived six years of wartime Poland in hiding. He wrote the following story while learning English in the study home "annex", Beatrice Carter's Newton home. It speaks for itself as it captures without complication Harry's needs and his assurance that they were being admirably met. Accounts of other refugee children would not be as uncomplicated.

"My Dog, Gorky"

One day, when I came back from the rest hour, Mrs. Carter told me that she had a big surprise for me. "Go, look under your bed." There was a little black puppy. He was very cute, but he was very afraid of people. He hid in a dark corner. When I was in the woods in Poland I was afraid. I knew how to help. I got down on the floor and took him on my lap. I said soft words to him and gave him food to eat.

When he lost his fear, he ran away from me. He played coming and going. Three boys could not catch him. He came to me to take a piece of candy. I held him and told him, "You go, but come back, because I love you and we are all safe in this house."

Four years after Harry wrote this, I, Mike, and other American children lived in that house. There we sought the same security and love that Harry required in his new life in America. With my Brownie Box camera I took a picture that I still possess. It is of

Mike and Burton playing on the front steps with a mature black cocker spaniel whose name you can surely guess.

ROBERT BERGER

Robert "Latzi" Berger's family was murdered in Auschwitz. He and an older brother survived four months there before liberation. He was sixteen when he arrived at Bradshaw House where he lived for a year (1947-'48).

Berger had achieved the equivalent of a seventh grade education In Hungary before the war. At Boston Latin School he completed a year's review course intended for returning G.I.'s. He did well on tests, impressed the right people, and was able to enroll as an undergraduate in Harvard University. "I was just lucky, lucky, lucky . . . at the right place at the right time," he told me. But I can easily read between the lines of his story that his intelligence and tenacity were critical to his good fortune.

We met in the lobby of a hotel near Boston and talked during breakfast in a quiet corner. I asked him, now retired from a long and distinguished career as a cardiac surgeon, if he had been "happy" in Bradshaw House. His answer was unequivocal: "No. We had food, which was much more important than it must have been to you [American children], because to us the most important thing was food. We had a roof over our heads . . . but I think we must have been really confused, lost, alone . . . But we had a goal—we wanted to move ahead—that was so powerful and overwhelming that I don't think I had time to think about whether I was happy or unhappy. That wasn't an issue. The issue was to survive and move ahead."

"You did that rather remarkably," I said.

"I think I did O.K.," he said.

Berger succinctly defined the roles played by Margolis and Carter in the agency's relationship to the refugee children. Margolis was "the main influence and a very powerful figure in the Jewish community . . . She could do things and get the Board to pay for all these things." His "impression" is that Carter, because of her influence upon Margolis, "was really the motivating force" behind the agency's excellent record of aiding the refugee children entrusted to it.

Although he was "not always welcome" in Carter's Newton home, Berger stayed there "off and on" during college vacations and attempted to supervise the dangerous and eccentric behavior of a disturbed boy named Danny Pietrowski. Because of this proximity to Carter and his own issues with her to deal with, he knew her well. She was "a Super Jew" who wasn't Jewish, Berger explained, a woman on a spiritual mission who chose to dress completely in white for shabat meals.

Carter, Berger continued, liked to tell how her father had been a Russian aristocrat murdered by Ukrainians in her presence. "Be brave," he had urged her with his dying breath, "and protect my [Jewish] people." Regardless of the anecdote's veracity, the story suggests the messianic and idiosyncratic character of her efforts on behalf of the Jewish children she indefatigably served. Combined, she and Margolis were an irresistible force. Berger "fell into their hands," but in his opinion it was Carter who was "essentially responsible for the by and large success of their relationship."

The phrase "by and large" suggests problems and problems there were, particularly with regard to Berger's powerful drive to obtain an education as it came up against Carter's conception of what was in his best interest. All who knew her will never forget her dynamic personality, but she could be arbitrary and hurtful in pursuit of her ends and the policies she shaped. As Berger said of his relationship with her and the agency, "It wasn't all gravy."

Berger must have been a remarkable and relentless teenager to achieve admission to Harvard after only a year in this country. With that accomplishment under his belt he went to Carter to request the agency's financial support. As he remembers it, their conversation went something like this:

"I want help."

"No, you must go to work, because the agency isn't going to support you."

[After a long discussion]: "I'm going to go to college."

"Maybe we could give you some advice."

"I don't need advice, I need money."

And that was the end of the conversation.

Berger found work on a construction site. Six weeks after their interview Carter called to offer him employment as a counselor at Camp Kingswood. Soon she agreed to some financial support from the agency. Although it was never enough, Berger learned that "there was no need to complain . . . It didn't help." Rather, he saw his situation as "an opportunity." When Carter denied him more money he replied, "I'll get my own." With some agency assistance as well as his earnings from the camp, waiting on table, working as a bellboy and chauffeur, and managing a sundries concession in the lobby of a Catskill hotel (of particular value to him and the late-night poker players from New York's Garment District), Berger made ends meet, earned a Harvard diploma, and enrolled in Boston University's School of Medicine.

Of Carter he said: "It was difficult to know her ways."

Of his relationship to the agency he said: "It was a mixed blessing, but by and large it was a blessing."

FEIGA HOLLENBERG CONNORS

Berger also said of Carter that "she had this talent of picking up people who were really hurting or needing . . . but sometimes it was too much." This observation certainly defines much of her relationship with Feiga Hollenberg.

Feiga had been "on the run" in Ukraine since she was seven but she was too weak to walk in snow near the war's end in Europe. Her father and brother left her with a Ukraine family and set out to find sanctuary for her and themselves. They were caught and murdered by peasants. Her mother and another brother, from whom the three had been separated, were already dead. Feiga was the only member of her family to survive the Holocaust. After the war she was gathered up with hundreds of other children under eighteen by the Hebrew Immigrant Aid Society. She was detained for a year and a half in a Displaced Persons camp until a visa could be obtained for her to enter the United States. She was fourteen when she arrived at Bradshaw House.

Feiga remains grateful today for the care she received there and at the Study Home, where she lived for a year. She is grateful, too, for the agency's "tolerance" of her emotional needs and its willingness to pay for her high school education at Windsor Mountain School in Lenox, Massachusetts. Feiga recalls that Carter "actively advocated" that she and other children be sent there by the agency.

Windsor Mountain was an alternative school staffed and attended by international teachers and students as well as by American students who relied on scholarships. Its roots were in Germany, where the Schule Marienau's founders, Max and Gertrude Bondy, emphasized multiculturalism and global stewardship. When the Nazis came to power the school was closed and the Bondys, who were Jews, were forced to emigrate, first to Switzerland and then to the U.S. There they began again, designing a school that was committed to the empowerment of its students, "a place, it asserted, where the children and young people in our care can develop in an atmosphere of freedom and mutual respect."

The school was a blessing for Feiga. She believes that by sending her there Carter and the agency "rescued" her from the many problems of teens and introduced her to a "non-demanding, non-threatening place where you could grow and put the past behind you." When asked, for the purpose of a recent reunion of alumni, what the school meant to her she answered: "The U.S. saved my life and Windsor Mountain saved my soul."

The school was not only a "very nice" place, in her opinion, but one that introduced her to an educational perspective that changed her life. She wanted a new life, she told me; she wanted not to live in the past; and she learned at Windsor Mountain that she need not be confined to living as "a European Jew," that she could identify with a larger group in "a humanitarian world."

Carter also encouraged Feiga to take advantage of psychiatric therapy at the agency's expense after her two years at Windsor Mountain. She did so and the experience, she explained when I met her and her husband in their Brookline home, "touched my heart." Her therapist had been a sympathetic Black woman whom Feiga, during the phenomenon of "transference," as she said, came to regard as her mother. That process taught her beyond any doubt that it is what one feels inside that matters.

Certainly the agency was sensitive to Feiga's feelings when it sponsored her two years at Windsor Mountain and provided the funds for her psychotherapy. Nevertheless, and despite Feiga's gratitude to the agency for nurturing her mental health, she was made to suffer by Carter's occasional but dramatic insensitivity to her emotional needs.

Feiga readily acknowledged Carter's good intentions when Carter insisted that she live in a foster home. She knew, too, that Carter had been actively involved in securing the best placement for her. But Feiga was unable to replace her own family with another, no matter how loving. "I had a home in my heart," she told me, one inhabited by her "wonderful family," her parents and younger brothers who had survived only in her memory. Carter did not appreciate the depth of that psychological reality and her intransigent commitment to the value of foster home care prevailed over Feiga's deep-seated reluctance to accept a foster family.

Feiga was "terrified" as she entered the Wax family and struggled with guilt throughout the year she lived with them. She believed she had made a contract with the Waxes upon joining their family and was "cheating" them every day by posing as the child they wanted when in fact she didn't want to be anyone's child. Feiga and her foster mother cried hard, together, as Feiga prepared to leave for the study home at the end of a relationship doomed from the start. (The agency soon sent the Waxes a four-year-old girl who could, indeed, be "theirs").

Like Berger, Feiga stayed in Carter's Newton home during school vacations and knew her well, knew her, in fact, to be an "erratic person" as surely as she was "giving." Both of these qualities were evident when Carter drove the two hours to Lenox and demanded that Feiga return with her to temple in Boston for the high-holiday services. When Feiga resisted Carter declared that she had inherited parental guardianship from her murdered parents and therefore must be obeyed. Feiga cried and surrendered to her feelings of rage and helplessness in the form of temper tantrums throughout the ride to Boston and for days afterward.

Feiga eventually enrolled in Boston University. With some early financial aid from the agency, work as a babysitter and nanny, and a scholarship she earned degrees in social work and began a career which led her to specialize in the treatment of autistic children.

Today, Feiga maintains that she has "nothing but the best feelings" for the agency and Carter and believes they "did everything an agency could do" to help her.

HELLA KAUFMAN WARTSKI

Hella Kaufman survived a year with her two sisters in Auschwitz and Freudenthal, a slave labor camp in Czechoslovakia. She writes in her testimony, dedicated to the memory of her parents: "For fifty years I have struggled with depression, shame, grief, and anger. I have feelings of anger for the murder of my parents and brother, the starvation, the destitution, the beatings, the fear and terror, the deprivation of liberty, the deprivation of human dignity and human kindness, the exploitation by slave labor, the denial of access to medication and education, and the denial of my belongings." After her liberation by Russian troops, two years residence in a D.P. camp in Germany, and an ocean voyage, Hella found herself a ward of the Jewish Family and Children's Service of Boston.

Hella lived in Bradshaw House for a year (1947-'48) and then, although she was "not too keen" on the idea, the agency placed her with a foster family. There she was miserable, consistently treated not as a beloved member of the family but as a maid and babysitter.

Hella phoned the agency office in tears one day. Carter answered her call, came immediately, quickly assessed the situation, and took Hella away. Because of that rescue, because Carter had responded so quickly and forcefully when called, Hella remained "very close" to her and "loved her dearly." She lived with her and Dora Margolis in Newton for the remaining months before the next academic year. Then the agency enrolled her in Windsor Mountain School.

Hella maintains that throughout the foster family ordeal she knew that the agency had attempted to do the right thing for her. Like Berger and Feiga, she frequently spent her vacation time in Newton. And like Berger's and Faiga's relationship with Carter, hers was sometimes marred by Carter's manipulative manner and insensitivity to her needs.

Eighteen, Hella met Heinz Wartski at Windsor Mountain and despite Carter's determined opposition the two planned to marry soon after they graduated. They did marry, defying Carter, and that spelled the end of Hella's educational expectations. She had been accepted at Wheelock College, in Boston, but was unable to attend because Carter vetoed the agency's financial support.

Hella remembers that Carter "felt sorry" for her after that episode and arranged for her to work as a housemother in the Study Home. She kept that position for two years, then taught nursery school for many more.

HEINZ WARTSKI

Heinz, too, was sent by the agency to Windsor Mountain; that was his sole relationship with the agency. He had escaped the Nazis during the war. His family had fled from Danzig and eventually found refuge with partisans in the hills of central Italy. After two years' living and working in Italy immediately after the war they lived for a year and a half in D. P. camps. They acquired financial aid from the Jewish Agency and obtained visas to enter the United States, choosing Boston as their destination because they were told that funds were available there for their assistance. They arrived, penniless, in Dorchester in January, 1949.

After a series of arduous and poorly paid factory jobs Heinz learned of the agency's existence. The result of that knowledge must have seemed to him a kind of miracle. Here is a passage excerpted from Heinz's memoir of his experience during the war and its aftermath. Beneath its unadorned recitation of facts we can discern Heinz's understanding that he and his brother had been given a gift of incalculable value, one that had become theirs for the asking.

> My father found out that the Jewish Family and Children's Service in Boston had sent other survivors of my age and my brother's age to private boarding schools and that we were also eligible to get into that program. He went to the director of the agency (Margolis) and complained that they should have informed us of this opportunity, and they didn't have the right to deprive us of this chance. The very next day, my brother and I were summoned to see the program director (Carter) who informed us about the private boarding schools that we were to attend, the weekly pocket money that we were to receive, the clothing they would buy for us and that the schools would take care of fitting us in scholastically.

The agency sent Max to the Cherry Lawn School in Darien, Connecticut, to complete his elementary education. Heinz was enrolled in Windsor Mountain. "After twelve years of absence from school I found it very rewarding," he wrote, "and it beat working in a factory. For me, this was a new world. This was the world of knowledge, and not of sweatshops or exploitation of labor."

After a year at Windsor Mountain Heinz decided to become an engineer. Twenty-one, he was no longer eligible for the agency's financial support. After military service in Korea he earned a degree from Northeastern University supported by the G.I. Bill, part time employment, and Hella's income as a nursery school teacher.

STEVE ROSS

When I first talked on the telephone to Szmulek and explained my purpose the first words he spoke were "I'm not angry with them." Of course I wondered what might have warranted anger on his part toward the agency that, by his own admission moments after his first words, had "made a difference in my life. I was so alone."

Szmulek was eight years old, one of his parents' eight children, when the Wehrmacht attacked Poland on September 1,1939. He survived the horrors of incarceration in a series of camps throughout the war until liberated from Dachau by American soldiers on April 29, 1945. One of those soldiers put his arm around Szmulek, a humane gesture that seemed extraordinary to Szmulek then and in the years to come. By war's end Szmulek's parents and six siblings had been murdered. His older brother, with whom he staggered out of Dachau, one falling, then the other, each helping his brother to stand, had become, in Szmulek's words, "a vegetable." Steve Ross is not Szmulek's given name. He had experienced and lost too much to continue being identified by it. In fact, he did not want to continue life as a Jew and discarded the name that proclaimed him one. Hospitalized and treated for tuberculosis, he lived in an orphanage and a D. P. camp, eventually traveling to New York City under the auspices of the American Committee for Orphaned Children. He was assigned to Philadelphia's Jewish Family and Children's Service, which later "mailed" him to Boston with a tag around his neck: "Boston JFCS".

Szmulek arrived at Bradshaw House at dinnertime with a small bag of belongings. He declined an invitation to join the boys and girls at the table and made his way to his designated bedroom. That room was also Robert Berger's, who climbed the stairs, entered, and found Szmulek sitting on a bed, eating bread and sausage. Robert asked him if he would like a glass of milk. Szmulek said yes. Robert brought it, and so began their life-long friendship.

As with Feiga, Hella, and Heinz, the agency sent Szmulek to Windsor Mountain School. But Szmulek believed it did so without enthusiasm, for Carter, whom Szmulek nevertheless remembers as having "a heart of gold," deemed him not to be "high school material" and approved financial support for only one year of his education in Lenox. Apparently she made little allowance for the fact that Szmulek had had no formal education, could neither read nor write in any language, and was, as he put it to me, "completely ignorant of the effects of education."

With "nowhere to go" after that year, Szmulek continued his education at Windsor Mountain for two years while employed by the school. He was responsible for operating six furnaces (with a bad back, broken in a camp for stealing a potato), cleaning the kitchen, and other janitorial duties. "I had to earn my keep," he said.

Szmulek was "very depressed" during his years at Windsor Mountain. He experienced the loss of his parents and siblings tremendously and felt "completely ostracized" from any notion of family. "I didn't want to live," he told me, weeping. He was lonely and confused, and "had no one coming to see me, no one to say a kind word to me, no one to say 'I love you.'" I asked him: Didn't you think Carter cared for you and the other agency wards? "I am sure she did, I am sure she did, but she didn't show it," he replied.

Szmulek emphatically claims that "no one gave me anything" so that he might attend college. He acknowledges his gratitude to the agency for the year's boarding school tuition and for the care at Bradshaw House, but insists that despite Carter and the other obstacles in his path toward a college education he succeeded by himself.

I conjecture that the source of any bitterness he might have harbored toward Carter and the agency lay not in its refusing him needed material aid, but in its reason for that refusal: Carter's lack of confidence in his abilities. Szmulek relates that his mother predicted he would be "a great man," and he was determined to realize that prophecy. His teachers at Windsor Mountain, too, recognized his intelligence and urged him to go to college. "I struggled with a tremendous amount of energy," Szmulek recalls, laboring "day and night" to earn the money he required. He pumped gas on Cape Cod, worked for a caterer and in a plastics factory "sometimes sixteen hours a day, seven days a week."

Throughout our extended phone conversations there was no mistaking Szmulek's pride in his abilities. He said, "I took a test and went to school and made something of myself." Regardless of Carter's negative assessment of his capacity—one that still stings, I feel, despite his assertion to the contrary—Szmulek forcefully declared, "I managed to make it and get on the dream."

Szmulek worked for forty years with inner city kids as a licensed psychologist employed by the City of Boston. He earned several degrees, including an honorary doctor of humanities from Northeastern for his work with children. Most important to him in recent years has been his dedication to one overarching task: "to get people to understand the incomprehensible," to understand the Holocaust, whose effects remain immediate in his life.

Szmulek still cries frequently. As he put it, "I am in mourning constantly, plagued by post traumatic stress syndrome." Although such a psychological state incapacitates many, it inspires Szmulek's "feverish" efforts to realize his mission. Accordingly, he was instrumental in persuading Boston's Mayor Ray Flynn to approve a project to build a Holocaust memorial in Boston. Without Szmulek's vision and ability to engage the mayor (who cried when Szmulek spoke to him of his Holocaust experience), to choose a site (one of five offered by the mayor), and to form "a committee of wonderful people" to get this memorial done, it would not have happened.

Today it is no wonder that Szmulek might feel some residue of anger when contemplating Carter's lack of confidence in him as well as the paucity of emotional support she offered. It is also a testament to his generous spirit that he denies it.

MICHAEL MOTYL

It was May 12, 1948. Mietek had stayed a month in the European-Jewish Children's Aid, Inc.'s Caldwell Avenue House in the Bronx. He took the subway to Grand Central Station where he boarded a train to South Station in Boston. There he presented a letter from the Children's Aid, Inc.'s director of placements to the Traveler's Aid Desk. It read: "This will introduce Mietek Motyl who is to go to the Jewish Family & Children's Service, 6 North Russell Street, Boston. We would appreciate it very much if you would place him in a cab with instructions to the driver to take him to the above address." That night Mietek slept in Bradshaw House.

Michael's journey to Dorchester had begun years before in the Warsaw and Parczew Ghettos. There he lost his mother who was caught in the first roundup of Jews sent to their deaths in Treblinka. By war's end his father had disappeared. Michael and his sister, as members of a forced labor brigade, were marched outside the walls but managed to slip away with the help of a Polish policeman their father had cultivated. Because they had blonde hair and green eyes they did not "look" Jewish and lived in hiding with Polish families during the rest of the war.

With the aid of a family friend after the war, Michael found himself in Lodz, a member of a kibbutz that planned to make its way to Palestine, where his sister had already gone. But an uncle who had survived the war in Russia removed him from there and sent him to Munich where he eventually obtained a visa to enter the United States.

In Munich, too, Michael was befriended by Szmulek. Both were so alone, Michael recalls, "but we had each other." They traveled together on the *Marine Marlin* to New York, Michael "as seasick as a dog," and arrived in April,1948.

The agency sent Michael to Camp Kingswood to adjust to his new culture and to learn English. He remembers the little plays the campers produced in that effort. In his free time he lobbied Beatrice Carter to arrange for Szmulek's transfer to the Boston agency. He succeeded and remembers seeing Szmulek's familiar face behind the car's window upon his arrival at camp.

Michael wanted to study at Windsor Mountain School, but was unsuccessful in obtaining the agency's sponsorship. He enrolled instead at Roxbury Memorial High School. Carter, he feels, exercised "a certain amount of arbitrariness" in determining this outcome. "She didn't think I was Jewish," Michael believes. "I didn't look Jewish."

After a year in the "safe, clean, friendly environment" of Bradshaw House, the agency placed Michael with a foster family in Brookline. Although life with Dr. Rand and his wife was sometimes "tense," Michael believes the family fared "as well as could be expected under the circumstances" when one considers how difficult it must be to find the "right elements" to ensure compatibility. He stayed with the Rands "for three or four" years, "until I could stand on my own feet." He managed to do so by all-night summer-work at a Sunoco station on Cape Cod (rooming with Szmulek) and employment at a Howard Johnson's restaurant in Hyannis.

Michael served in the army, earned a degree from Boston University, and rose from a trainee in a subsidiary of Container Corps of America to an executive position with Mobil Oil. He lives with his wife in Florida and travels to visit his three children and their families.

PETER KOLBE

When I review the notes I took during two lengthy phone conversations with Peter Kolbe an image forms in my mind, distant but persistent. A solitary little boy dressed in a thin black coat runs around and around in circles in the schoolyard across from the Ladies Helping Hand Home. He is running because it is a raw winter day and he is cold.

It is 1941. The boy lives with several children in the big, white house across the street but he doesn't want to be there. He cries frequently and spends "a lot of time trying to forget what was going on" in his life. In fact, much of his childhood would be spent not wanting to be in places where he found himself. These included pre-war Vienna, the Ladies Helping Hand Home in Brighton, and Bradshaw House.

Peter's mother and father told him that he could not have remembered Kristallnacht, that he was only two and a half that November evening in 1938, too young to do so. But Peter says he still remembers his fear as stones crashed through his bedroom window. Throughout the next year his parents tried everything to get out of Austria within the quota established for Jewish émigrés and had the good luck to succeed, although they were forced to leave Peter's grandmother behind.

The Kolbes lived in Chelsea, just across the bay from Boston, and struggled to make ends meet. Peter's father's hands were increasingly crippled by arthritis, and his mother suffered from physical and psychological problems. Consequently, their day-to-day existence was precarious.

The question became "What shall we do with Peter?" By his own admission he was "a mama's boy." At age three a supervisory arrangement with his "aunt" failed to compensate for his mother's absence. At four kindergarten could not staunch his tears. "They kicked me out," Peter recalls, "because I cried all the time." As a last resort his parents found a home for him with the Ladies Helping Hand Auxiliary. Although they came to visit every weekend, Peter cried much of the time during their visits. Living without his mother at the age of five was "devastating". It was as if "his whole world crashed."

There were some things he liked in Brighton: the donuts the cook made every Sunday morning; riding a tricycle on the long, tarred driveway. He readily accepted the jobs assigned to him, like setting the table for meals and making up his bed. But most of his memories of the Brighton home "are not very good:" the large bedroom and his cot, but never a permanent feeling of the cot's being "his"; the embarrassing knowledge that he never had proper clothes; the empty feeling of being friendless; the near-sleepless nights lying in the dark, fearing another sickening episode of a boy's trying to get into bed with him. In short, he "didn't want to be there at all." Peter characterizes his experience in the Brighton home as "a disaster." He lived there for four years.

Nine years old, Peter returned to his parents' apartment and lived there beyond the time his mother entered Jewish Memorial Hospital. She would die there two and a half years later. Peter's relationship with his father is summed up in a few words: "He didn't talk to me, I didn't talk to him." It was probably his father who contacted the successors of the Ladies Helping Hand Auxiliary, for without his wife and with the need to work he could not care properly for his son. The agency sent Peter to Camp Chebacco, by a lake in Essex, Massachusetts, and then to Malden to live with the Goldbergs, whom Peter remembers as "a very nice family."

But in Peter's experience there were no friends to be made in Malden and his caseworker judged that he would be better off living with boys his age. After six months with the Goldbergs Peter, at fourteen, found himself living at Bradshaw House.

There things "turned out to be fun" in some ways. Although Peter made only one real friend, Izzy Milkow, Bradshaw House contained a social life in which he gladly participated. There were the ordinary interpersonal relationships of boys living together as family, and the special occasions, like the dances with neighborhood girls or the girls from Brighton, occasions upon which Peter learned how to interact with other children.

But Peter was not happy at Bradshaw House, either. He wasn't doing his homework and consequently had to transfer from the prestigious Boston Latin School to English High. He resented the small amount of time his caseworkers spent with him, and he was upset by the requirement that he go to them in Boston's West End—that "they didn't come to me." He recalls that Beatrice Carter was "the boss" at Bradshaw House, supervising the caseworkers who had business with boys there and playing a definitive role in the House's management. In Peter's opinion she favored her pets, particularly one whom she sent to Windsor Mountain, leaving Peter to take the "T" to his urban high school, as well as to North Russell Street to collect his allowance and to "report in." Most troubling was his relationship with his housefather, Maury.

The two were not a good match. Maury's personality was loud, aggressive, and domineering. Peter rarely spoke and was shy, so reserved that he was afraid to enter stores. He tried to avoid Maury, but Maury apparently felt a need to bring Peter out of himself. It was an uneven contest. Peter felt only threat from Maury. He perceived all his shouted words and orders to be personal attacks and he hated him for them. Looking backward, Peter admits that Maury might have succeeded in making him less shy and more aggressive, if only to protect himself from his tormenter. But when I suggested that Maury's coarse manner might have been purposeful, a crude but well-intentioned strategy arrived at by caseworkers, Mrs. Carter, and other houseparents, Peter said no, he didn't think so, for after Maury left no trace of that behavior remained.

Peter lived in Bradshaw House until he was sixteen, when he returned home to help his father. He went on to earn a degree in Engineering from Northeastern University and eventually made a career selling engineering equipment. As a salesman he must have conquered his fear of people and he acknowledges that his trials, in general, made him "a stronger individual." To what extent the agency aided that growth is anybody's guess.

IZZY MILKOW

Israel Milkow's schoolboy account of Bradshaw House, which I present in full, is included in his memoir, *Gedenkt mine kind, ver du binst* (Remember my child, who you are). Some knowledge of his remarkable journey to Dorchester and beyond is necessary if we are to understand who Izzy is and what role the agency played in shaping that identity.

Izzy was five years old when he was separated from his doomed parents and four brothers as the Germans invaded southern Poland. He fled east with his uncle and several members of his extended family. Their flight ended in Samarkand, in Uzbekistan, where Izzy lived in a Soviet orphanage throughout the remainder of the war. By war's end his uncle and all of his family were dead, victims of typhus, malaria, and Soviet work camps.

Sent back to Poland with thousands of orphaned children, Izzy was recruited by a kibbutz to travel to Palestine. "That was my happiest time," he writes of his association with the young Zionists. "I was no longer afraid of the people in charge of me. I was with my own group . . . I was among my own people and it was good." But after a trek over the Alps to Italy sickness intervened and Izzy was left behind.

While in a D.P. camp in Rome he was recruited by a Hassidic religious group and an ultra-religious yeshiva. "For about three and a half years," Izzy writes, "I was a Yeshiva Bocher." It was unimportant whether or not he believed in that life. "The important thing was that I was part of an organization. I was part of them, they were part of me, and we got along. I felt safe and secure, protected. I had my place to stay, I had my friends, I had food on the table and there was learning going on."

Izzy had found a home.

He traveled with the yeshiva to Montreal, but returned alone to Italy in pursuit of a visa to enter the United States. An aunt there had seen his name published with the names of other survivors in the *Daily Jewish Forward* and began what would become a lengthy and arduous legal process to bring Izzy to Dorchester. But Izzy felt homeless once more. His American relatives "had started to unravel my life again" by taking him out of the yeshiva. "Right there they uprooted me from what basically had been my home and school. What I had lived with and knew."

The Jewish Family and Children's Service of Montreal assisted Izzy for as long as he remained in Canada. In 1950 he was finally allowed to enter the U.S. There his experience with his various family members grew traumatic. Some insisted that he continue a religious life, others that he assimilate to the secular American culture. When he could not commit to one or the other way of life his relatives didn't know what to do with him. They became estranged from him and from each other. Izzy was unhappy in their homes and was made increasingly uncomfortable by their demands and the ugly inter-family squabbles regarding his future. It was then that one relative referred Izzy to the agency. Soon he was living in Bradshaw House.

I conclude this synopsis of Izzy's memoir with a fragment of his account of life in the Soviet orphanage. It depicts the uprooted and near-homeless nature of his eleven years' odyssey, and like so much in his account, makes obvious his physical and emotional need for a place to call home.

> Sometimes when I look back and I talk about it, I feel that for those of us who survived, it really was a miracle . . . The mattresses and pillows in the children's home were made out of straw. There were no beds. We slept on the mattresses lined up on the floor one next to another. We had army blankets. Each child had a place to sleep. You had a little place just to put your head there . . . I don't think that we each had our own little place so that we could sleep every night in the same place. There was no privacy . . . During the day the mattresses were piled up one on top of the other so that the hall could be used during the daytime as a place where we ate our meals and had some kind of schooling. I do remember that in the morning, especially from the smaller children, the mattresses would be taken out to be dried and then later in the late afternoon or evening the mattresses would be brought back in and they would be dry and we could go to sleep. You would not have the same mattress from night to night. It did not matter if it was clean or dirty or who had used it before. You could see the stains on the mattresses. You could see everything.

What must life in Bradshaw House have meant to a boy who had experienced this and much worse?

Here are Izzy's schoolboy impressions of Bradshaw House and its role in his life. He composed them as he learned English at the Kingsley School, a preparatory school in Boston whose tuition was paid by the agency.

What Bradshaw House Means to Me

by
Israel Milkow

Before I write what Bradshaw House means to me, I would like to give you a picture of the inside and outside appearance of the house and what Bradshaw House is.

Chapter I

The Inside and Outside Appearance
of Bradshaw House

At this time, Bradshaw House consists of twelve boys, a director and his wife, an assistant, a cook and a janitor. This house is found in Dorchester. The appearance of the house is very pretty. I would say that it is the prettiest house in the street. Coming to the house you see flowers and trees all around. The house is painted white. There is a small white fence which was made by the boys. This fence encloses the flowers. There is also a small garden where tomatoes, squash, peppers, lettuce, and beans are growing. The boys like to take care of the gardens and to water them. Around the back of the yard is a large white fence which was built by the boys last year. Not far from the garden is a large white cement block which was made by the boys also. This is for the Ping-Pong table and there is a large wooden wall built so that the boys could play a favorite ball-game called, "King". Painted on the cement is a Shuffleboard Court and a Baseball game which the boys play when they are not using the Ping-Pong table. Nearby are some red and white chairs and a table on the grass for the boys to relax after playing these games. This is more or less the appearance of the house from the outside.

Now we will go around to the front as though we were walking into the house. In front of the steps are white bricks placed one in front of the other. Going into the house you come to the reception hall. From there you see the living room which looks like it belonged to a very aristocratic house. There is a nice sofa, chairs, a television set, little tables with lamps on each one. The floor is nicely waxed. On the left side there is a library, a bookcase with books and on the top shelves there are model airplanes, ships and cars which were made by different boys in the house and each one puts his model on the shelves.

Going upstairs we come to the bedrooms and the office. The rooms are very pretty and two or three boys are in each one. Each week we change the sheets which means that all the beds are always clean.

This is a little of the inside and outside of the house. Now there is a great deal to write but I leave this for the next time.

Chapter II

What Bradshaw House Is

As you already know from my first story what the inside and outside of Bradshaw House is like, we will now go to Chapter Two, what Bradshaw House is.

This is a house like other houses but with another purpose . . . Bradshaw House has a great responsibility on it. It has a great deal to accomplish and much of it has already been done. We can say that Bradshaw House is a small family for different boys from different places. New Americans and old Americans . . . it is for boys who have to have help in different ways. They need help some with education, some with a place to live, and some to learn to live with other people. With these things their parents cannot help them. Here they also have the opportunity to go to special schools for help. Here in Bradshaw House the children get a warm feeling that people care for them even more than just to see that they have good food to eat, a good place to sleep and a chance to get an education.

Chapter III

What Bradshaw House Means to Me

As you are now familiar with both of my chapters describing Bradshaw House, you will be able to understand easier what Bradshaw House means to me. I would like to give you a little information about my life so you can see how important Bradshaw House is to me.

I was born in Poland. When the war began in 1939, I escaped to Russia with my uncle. There I was for five years and I struggled in a Russian Children's Home, not knowing about life or what life is, not having anything to eat, and living like an animal, trying to figure out how to get away from there and to go back home to Poland. God helped me and I was able to get away and go back to Poland. But having left Russia, I came to another Russian country in Poland. Then I tried to figure out how to leave there and go somewhere else. I came to Italy and also there it was not a good place for me. I tried to come to America and it took a long time. It was very hard for me.

Now, Thank God, I am in America and am at Bradshaw House. Now, can you imagine the wonderful place that I have found after wandering for eleven years over the whole world. It is very hard for me to describe all the things which I have suffered through. I hope you can understand me. Now you can understand what kind of a place I found when I came here to Bradshaw House. Now I can tell you that Bradshaw House means for me a mother and a father that worry about their child and try to give them the best things that they can give them. This is a house for me where I feel like in my own home. I am free. This is the first house where I have felt so good since I left my own home. The house is dear to me. I know that it is my present and my future home. The house will help me as long as I need help. I believe that I will never forget the warm welcome that Bradshaw House has given to me.

I remember the building named Bradshaw House, inside and out, as an unadorned and utilitarian place. Izzy's much grander perception of its physical features has everything to do with the degree of his homelessness when compared to mine, and the duration of his desire to be cared for in a home whose stability he could rely upon. Yet despite the experiential gap that lay between us, when we met with our wives to share a meal at Rein's Deli, near Hartford, I sensed that we were kindred spirits insofar as Bradshaw House's capacity to satisfy our needs for family and security was concerned.

Izzy "felt at home" during the year (1950-'51) he lived at Bradshaw House. The boys "all got along nicely." He and his housemates hiked, camped, hosted parties with the neighborhood girls, and enjoyed arts and crafts. Izzy still has the Passover plate on which he painted and glazed a pomegranate. He met with his caseworker "at least once a week," troubled in particular by increasingly difficult relations with his relatives.

By the next academic year Izzy was enrolled in Roxbury Memorial High School. Although he sometimes walked over to visit his friends, Bradshaw House was no longer Izzy's home. The agency had placed him in a nearby foster home. The Holtzmans were elderly and "strictly business people," with no warmth to share with their new boarder. "I had a room there and they fed me," Izzy wrote. He did not understand why he had been taken again from his home and "put in that kind of atmosphere . . . but I was." Gradually, however, Izzy began to determine his own orbit: to make his own money, to think and act for himself, and to become independent of the agency, the Holtzmans, and his relatives. An employer whom he cared for took him in and treated him as family.

Izzy wanted to study at Yeshiva University after graduation from high school but the agency declared him ineligible for its financial assistance because his family had the money to support his education. His ambition came to nothing, however, because his relatives, nursing their grievances, would not pay. "After all," Izzy acidly remarked, "according to them, I was not supposed to have any feelings."

Izzy considers himself to be a fortunate man. He graduated from the Hebrew College in Newton, taught Hebrew for thirty years, and now works as a data processor for a large firm near Boston. Most importantly, he has a devoted wife and two children, a family to which he can belong and the ability to protect and care for them. "My wife," he says, "tells me that I've done a good job."

Robert Berger's judgment that the relationship between these European refugees and Boston's Jewish Family and Children's

Service "wasn't all gravy" is certainly confirmed by their personal accounts. Several children dependent upon the agency's support ran afoul of Carter's erratic personality and arbitrary judgments, particularly with regard to their foster home placements and the financial support for education they did or did not receive. These were areas over which Carter possessed an absolute authority within the agency. At the same time, many of those hurt by Carter's apparent insensitivity to their needs claim to have loved her for her fierce determination to do what was right for them as she saw it. Her "heart of gold," as Szmulek put it, beat for these Jewish children.

These accounts reveal the strength that allowed boys and girls to rise above their circumstances and to live productive lives. But they didn't do it alone. Regardless of the pain or discomfort they experienced in the process of reconstructing their fractured lives, pain sometimes caused by the agency, itself, and despite the fact that the manner of support was sometimes seriously flawed, they were fortunate that the agency was there with its food and lodging and clothing, its financial support, its abundant caring and its determination to do the right thing by these children. If the relationship between the new Americans and the agency was, again in Robert Berger's words, a "mixed blessing" it was, "by and large, a blessing."

And as I pause and take my fingers from the keyboard and consider what I have just written, I recognize that Berger's final judgment might well be identical to mine and Mike's. The quality of agency care for us was compromised by two serious flaws: its failure to pursue attempts to help us deal with our deep-seated distress, and its choice of our first foster home. As I have written, I believe the agency's overall success in nurturing us, American and refugee alike, was due primarily to the exacting casework standards applied to our circumstances, standards shaped and insisted upon by Carter. Her approach to the refugee children, however, was more complex, more problematic than it was to us because she applied to them a more intensely personal, messianic, and consequently more rigid version of those standards.

The following anecdote suggests the remarkable intensity of Carter's devotion to her European charges:

Edith Zimmerman was Feiga's roommate while each studied at Boston University's School of Social Work. She never forgot the impression Carter made upon her as a kind of elemental force. During our telephone conversation Edith recalled that she was working toward her Master's degree and serving as an aide at the prestigious McLean's Hospital, near Boston, where she knew Danny Pietrowski. Danny was an extraordinarily demanding patient who had been referred to the hospital by the agency. He was "sexually precocious," "a terror," and "dangerous," according to Edith, feared at fourteen by grown men for his strength and unpredictability. Edith was on duty when Carter stormed onto the ward, strode to Danny's room, and "whisked him away." She was dissatisfied with the treatment Danny was receiving.

This was a woman whom anyone would want in his corner regardless of her capacity to dismay. All of us—European and American alike—were fortunate that she was.

APRIL 1, 1950, SEDER FOR NEW AMERICANS:
LEONARD SERKESS AT FAR LEFT,
BEATRICE CARTER AT REAR RIGHT

Becoming Adults

I have always associated my development from a dependent child to a young adult in charge of my own decisions with the aroma of new mown grass.

I am walking alone down the steep hill from Butterfield, my dormitory at the University of Massachusetts. The day is blue and green and suffused by an August haze. I can see the Student Union building and College Pond and the Old Chapel and a tractor moving slowly in wide arcs as it cuts acres of grass with its extended mowing arm.

I know almost no one among the freshmen gathered here for orientation.

I am on my own, hours and miles from my father, my brother, my foster family, my caseworker, and I am elated by my newly found independence.

Although I do not think of it at the moment, I know that I would not be here without the agency's personal and financial support. And as far as independence goes, the agency has worked hard, like a good parent, to foster that spirit, to encourage me to do as much as I can by myself and then to count on its help when I need it.

Nowhere is this policy more apparent than in the agency's role in my achieving a university education.

Mike's academic performance in high school dissuaded him from attempting a four-year college program. He completed a two-year Business program at Burdett College in Boston. But if the content of our educational experiences differed markedly, the agency taught each of us identical lessons regarding the value of a mature independence. As we began to consider post-high school education it insisted that we do all we could financially to support ourselves.

That is why it would be imprecise to say that the agency paid for our educations. The case notes from the last years of our relationship with the agency rarely concern our academic progress without also considering our jobs, our savings, our ability to assume responsibility for an increasing array of our needs until, at the last, we were paying for much of our expenses—and almost liking it.

I began my first job, at Hamm's Ice Cream Parlor, in the fall of my sophomore year at Winthrop High School. My foster mother and caseworker were pleased, but not nearly as much as I, whom my caseworker, Paul Dubroff, described as "very excited." I had been "feeling the pinch of not having enough spending money," and waiting on customers seated on stools at a soda fountain seemed a pleasant way to earn money three hours a day, three days a week.

I deposited my earnings with regularity into my new savings account and treasured the beige booklet in which the bank tellers stamped evidence of my money's incremental growth. Rowie was initially disturbed that I was hoarding my money and she "had the feeling" that I was depending upon the agency for my weekly allowance despite my changed financial circumstances. I imagine these concerns were valid at first, but I soon relieved her of both. I drew upon my savings to buy a portable Underwood typewriter and an aquarium for tropical fish. (I can see with my mind's eye the precise shade of the typewriter's blue and the bright kingdom I created for my tiger barbs and neon tetras).

My expectation of a continued allowance from the agency was disappointed when I spoke to Dubroff, who explained that as I was earning my own money it was "only fair" that I pay for personal expenses out of my own pocket. I kept to myself what reservations I had about such logic and impressed Dubroff by my "accepting of the idea." Rowie, too, acknowledged that I was learning to manage my affairs and was "turning out" well.

Mike's response to similar circumstances was more honest than mine. He, too, "had been having considerable difficulty stretching his money to include baseball games, movies and the like." Consequently, he reasonably suggested to Dubroff that his allowance be increased. Dubroff pointed out to him that he was already receiving $1.25 a week, the maximum allowance from the agency for a boy his age. "Most fellows," he added, "got thinking about getting part time work to supplement their allowance." Mike "put up an objection to this" and made it clear that he preferred to dedicate his free time to basketball.

Months after that interview Rowie reported to Dubroff that all of Mike's friends had jobs but Mike "preferred not to look" for one. He was acquiring bad habits, she said, borrowing from his friends and me and not paying us back. Dubroff felt "it was very important to M.'s development that he find a job and have some experience of his own self working, being able to earn money for his own labor." Although Dubroff pressed this logic upon Mike on several occasions it was not until the start of Mike's junior year that he succumbed to "a good deal of pressure" from Rowie and Dubroff and applied for a paper route.

"There is a good deal of dependency in this boy," Dubroff concluded, "which was seen in the way in which he delayed real efforts on looking for a job. He seems to express the attitude that the agency is made of money and all he need do is ask." Despite this assessment Dubroff believed Mike was "handling his adolescence fairly well." Rowie thought him "loveable with a fine sense of humor but too carefree and irresponsible." He was a "sports fanatic," she said, interested wholly in athletics to the neglect of his schoolwork. In his junior year of high school, he showed no concern for his future. Rowie and Dubroff agreed that more prompting by them and psychological testing to determine Mike's vocational aptitudes were in order.

In contrast to Mike, I had always been a successful student, a perennial member of the honor roll. In Mike's opinion, as he often put it, "Ben got the brains." Agency staff assumed that I would go on to college, and just after my junior year of high school Dubroff and I "took up the subject." That year I had earned straight B's, increased my working hours, and paid for all my personal expenses. When he considered my earnings from Hamm's, from a prospective job that summer as a camp counselor, and from part time employment at UMass, Dubroff had "little question" that I would be able to contribute "substantially" to my college expenses. When he passed my case to Herman Steingraph, the caseworker who would see Mike and me through our final years with the agency, Dubroff remarked upon the growth I had already realized: "He has come to be able to stand on his own feet and looks more to himself for [his] needs."

I met with Steingraph in his office to discuss "academic planning" and hastily agreed "that if the agency were to help [me] I would have to do all possible [myself] to gain the necessary money for [my] education." But Steingraph believed I had complied too easily with this fundamental requirement. I had been "quite vague" regarding my financial resources, estimated expenses, and sources of scholarship aid to which I had applied. Steingraph and Estelle Cross, his supervisor, decided to wait for me to provide a full account of these points "before delving into the matter of agency aid."

The thoroughness with which I prepared that account in mid-May,1958, (typed, single spaced, one and a half pages) reveals my enhanced understanding that this was serious business and I had better be on top of it. I understood that the agency would not allow me to take its financial support for granted.

The agency approved its underwriting of my UMass education within a month of receiving my financial statement. When he relayed the news with his congratulations to me Steingraph could not resist asking if I intended to acquire a part time job at the University. In his office to arrange for payment of fees, we determined I had $300 of my own. "Books and laundry fee would take care of $110. The remaining $190 would be used for incidental clothing, travel, and recreation during the first semester." Once we had agreed upon these and other financial details, Steingraph turned with admiration to my heavy academic load: French, History, English, Psychology, Botany, ROTC, Speech and Physical Education.

This pattern remained consistent throughout my years at UMass. As professionally interested as Steingraph was in my personal and academic life (he was in regular contact with my ill and indigent father at the time, and always asked for news of my college life), he usually expressed that interest in close company with the details of my financial circumstances. There was never a *quid pro quo* arrangement that the agency's continued support depended upon my satisfactory academic performance, but there was always the expectation that I, and not the agency, be responsible for the expenses I could reasonably manage.

Steingraph embodied in these financial matters my understanding of the agency as humane and dispassionate, one whose expectations were coming to be my own. For instance, when he turned down my request for $20 for books because I had not properly budgeted my funds and because books came under the heading of personal expenses, he asked if I were "a little sore or angry" because of this rejection. I shook my head, he reported, and said that I planned to do as much as I could for myself, that I didn't want to take much from the agency, that I wanted to be "as self-sufficient as possible."

My progress to this new level of maturity was inconsistent. At the start of my senior year I was apparently "a little forgetful," as Steingraph delicately described my conduct, of the arrangement that I would pay for all expenses other than tuition, board, and room. I had sent him a bill from my linen service for the previous academic year. "The agency has seen fit to pay this in the past," I wrote, "and as my purchasing of my entire wardrobe is going to stretch my intricate budget pretty thin, I hope they, at the agency, will take care of it again." The following is Steingraph's response:

Dear Ben:

Concerning your request for payment of laundry fees, I believe this is something you are able to take care of yourself at this time. I have considered this request in the light of your available and anticipated funds. I believe you would be able to manage the fee and have sufficient funds (and then some) for clothing purchases.

In the past, when we have paid your laundry fee, I recall that your financial situation was more strained than is the case now.

Let me assure you that I carefully consider your financial resources in relation to any needs that arise for you.

Sincerely yours,
Herman Steingraph,
Caseworker

Humane. Dispassionate. When I saw Steingraph later that month I told him I had not been surprised by his rejection of my request, but thought it worth a try. Undismayed, I voiced my wish to save money to buy a second-hand car in my senior year. Steingraph reminded me that I would first have to meet my obligation to pay for all personal expenses, including my clothes. Despite temptation, there was no escape from agency expectations.

In order to meet those expectations I worked throughout my four years at UMass, as a dishwasher and server in my dorm's cafeteria for three and as a soda jerk in a downtown Amherst restaurant during my senior year. I also worked during every summer and during some vacations: as camp counselor, manager of a yacht club's food concession, and part-time manager of a downtown Boston coffee house, among other jobs. I saved enough money by the end of my junior year to meet my financial obligations. (But there would be no car).

Regardless of its insistence that I be responsible for all my personal expenses the agency willingly paid for some when it understood I could not. For instance, I had only $50 in my savings account after my first semester at UMass, most of which was already targeted for books and other necessaries. I would be earning $110 during the next semester, but it appeared I would need $75-$85 more to cover expenses. Steingraph told me he would submit these facts to his supervisor and "hopefully" he would be able to send me a check, which he did, for $75. By June I had no money with which to carry myself through my summer employment at Camp Chebacco. Steingraph figured that $35 should be sufficient, received approval for this amount, and sent me the check. In fact, when Steingraph told me of the agency's refusal to pick up the $20 tab for my purchase of books during my sophomore year, he added that I should try to find the money, but if I could not to contact him and he would do what he could for me.

If, as Steingraph observed, I seemed to feel at the start of my college career that the agency would give me anything I wanted, by the fall term of my senior year I was paying for all my personal expenses, including all my clothes, and for all my meals. Agency financial support ended completely upon my 21st birthday in early February. Although I resented the abruptness of the severance of financial support I understood that it was consistent with agency policy. With savings from my post-graduate summer job I paid off the student loan I had needed to finance my final semester at UMass. I was excited and feeling confident. No small amount of those feelings was due to my having been well prepared by the agency to live self-sufficiently.

Steingraph also encouraged Mike to work toward independence and quickly understood the complexity of the task. Early in their relationship Mike struck him, as he had Dubroff, as a particularly dependent boy who wished "to evade decision-making and assumption of responsibility." He conjectured that Mike had, perhaps, "let himself be submerged by his brother's accomplishments . . . in effect preventing him from being able to plan for himself." Steingraph acknowledged by letter to Mike that he very likely was anxious about his post-high school education and asked him to come into his office and talk. Mike did and a discussion about basketball broke the ice that lay between them. They met every three weeks during the following months and discussed, among other topics, reasons for optimism regarding Mike's future. Mike expressed interest in studying Business after high school, and he was positive about the prospect of vocational aptitude testing.

As the fall term of his senior year progressed, Mike told Steingraph that "he felt more and more the need to make a decision, to initiate planning." He understood, as Steingraph put the matter to him, that in doing so he would be assuming a degree of personal responsibility, as he had in his finding employment at Hamm's, his first steady job as it had been mine. He was already working several hours a week and paying for all his personal expenses. Mike eagerly anticipated the results of his vocational testing, but agreed with Steingraph "that tests could indeed be helpful, but he, himself, would have to be comfortable with a choice." By April he had chosen to apply to Burdett and had come to terms with the financial arrangements insisted upon by the agency. "He understands," Steingraph recorded, "that school financing by the Agency will be made relative to his own resources." In May Burdett approved Mike's application and Mike told Steingraph that he could now "hold his head high."

Despite Mike's significant progress, however, Steingraph knew there remained considerable room for growth. On the one hand, Mike had "been able to mobilize his anxiety about his status sufficiently to . . . move on his own to attain his goals—not only following suggestions." But on the other hand there were many indications of his passivity in his relationships to adults.

Steingraph was particularly interested in Mike's failure to tell him that he did not want to proceed with the orthodontic treatment that had been recommended several years before. He asked Mike why he had failed to keep his appointments with the doctor. Mike replied that he did not want to say no to Steingraph, that he felt obligated to the agency and had to this point always done what they had told him to do. After this disclosure Steingraph focused during their regular meetings upon Mike's feelings toward authority. He began with the premise that Mike should "*feel* that he doesn't have to please the agency at all times." Orthodontic treatment was cancelled.

Mike had saved almost $200 by the time his first semester at Burdett approached. He and Steingraph agreed that he would be able to pay for his personal expenses, including his books and much of his clothing. He vowed to work hard at school and Steingraph assured him that the agency had "every expectation" that he would succeed and would "stand in back of him financially and otherwise during his school career."

Mike's deserved feelings of growing maturity proved difficult to maintain when he found himself treated as if he were an irresponsible child. Steingraph reported with some astonishment the "little difficulty" Mike experienced after he got a job at a soda fountain in an amusement arcade in downtown Boston. The job fit in well with his academic schedule. He could go there directly from classes at 2:00 and work for $1 an hour until 6:30, when he would return to Winthrop, eat, and do his homework. It was especially desirable in that it left him completely free for basketball on weekends. Rowie, however, was upset.

Steingraph learned of Rowie's concern from Dubroff, then his supervisor, whom Rowie had irately telephoned. She did not think Mike should work in so terrible a place. She had "got on Mr. Gordon's ear" regarding the unsuitability of such a job for Mike, and had apparently gone herself to speak her mind to the employer. In the end Mike was laid off, which left him without a job and with considerable embarrassment, particularly when our Aunt Minnie, who had been alerted by our father, came to Winthrop and berated Rowie for her handling of the matter. At first she, too, had been upset, she admitted, but soon understood that all Mike wanted was to make money and that he had no contact with the shady people at the amusement center. Too late for Mike, Rowie came to think the job "a pretty good idea." She and Irv pressed Mike "in no uncertain fashion" to stop his moping and find another job.

Steingraph met Mike by chance in the subway at this time and thought him "rather blue and a little depressed" about his employment situation. But he was working with a Burdett counselor to find another job and was soon at work again, in the stockroom of a Boston clothes manufacturing firm at $1.25 an hour. "Thus, his monetary needs were being taken care of pretty fully," Steingraph concluded. His self-confidence, however, had sustained some bruising from the episode.

Mike's dependence was "obvious" to Steingraph after his first semester at Burdett. He remarked that "this boy" required "a well-structured situation" in which to function well. Mike, himself, had suggested that he continue to meet with Steingraph every three weeks, and that he foresaw the need to maintain that contact after he had graduated. Steingraph assured him that he would not simply drop out of the picture, that he wanted to continue to help him, but that this help "would be with the focus of Mike doing more and more on his own." They then reviewed what Mike had done already: having a part-time job, paying for his own clothes, paying for his own books, and taking care of his personal expenses in general. But Mike remained anxious about his capacity to succeed after Burdett and joked that if the agency wanted to pay for his board in Winthrop until he was sixty, "that's okay, too."

Like me, Mike sometimes attempted to evade the agency's exacting standards. At the close of an interview with Steingraph in June of his senior year of high school he asked if the agency would pay to Burdett the $40 registration fee. "How much money do you have in the bank, Mike?" Steingraph asked. The conversation soon ended with Mike's admission that because he had a job and savings $40 was a sum "he could well afford to take care of himself." Steingraph pointed out that Mike's paying the bill with his own money would amount to "his own personal commitment to his education." Mike left the office "a bit unhappy with this arrangement" despite his grudging approval of the principle behind it. He must have understood that his freedom to disagree with the agency did not mean that the agency would necessarily see things his way.

Another incident, mid-way through his second year at Burdett, is still more suggestive of Mike's dependence at that time and the agency's response to it. He had failed a course in Insurance but had done nothing to ascertain that fact's impact upon his overall academic status. Steingraph told him "very strongly" that he had better follow up on the matter with the school. Mike did and learned that he would have to repeat the course in order to graduate. That would cost $45. "M. wondered whether or not we could pay this," Steingraph reported, "but I outlined for M. the fact that this problem had arisen because he had not done the work and he should certainly pay." This attempt to evade the consequences of his irresponsibility seems to me the nadir of my brother's journey toward independence. But even then two difficult circumstances were conspiring to turn him in the right direction.

Our father collapsed in an alcoholic stupor and had to be taken to the hospital after Mike's first semester at Burdett. At the same time the issue of one of us having to leave our foster home was put on the table, discussed and resolved. Steingraph understood that Mike "certainly" did not want to move from the stable home environment the E.s provided. He and Rowie "felt . . . that Ben was far better able to leave her home than was Mike." Mike would stay, but Steingraph made it clear, with Mike's concurrence, that when he obtained a full time job he would be responsible for paying the cost of his room and board and would be "a free agent completely in an economic sense." (Eventually, Mike would live and prosper for several years in a basement room in Winthrop. He would find love and security with the E.s until the day he married).

Steingraph developed a persuasive hypothesis with regard to our father's deterioration and its connection to Mike's growth: Mike's repeated insistence during several interviews that he wanted to wash his hands of his father was a reflection of the "tremendous" fear that he might eventually be as helpless as his father, that he, too, might be a failure. Steingraph surmised that to a boy who desperately wanted "some measure of economic security and success," rejection of the father represented rejection of the fear. Having listened to this hypothesis and determined to have no further contact with his father, "M. outwardly seemed to feel a lot better" and the depression that Steingraph had seen in him "lifted considerably."

Mike pulled away "quite noticeably" from the agency in the following year, Steingraph wrote in December of 1961. Established with the E.s and estranged from his father and what his father represented to him, he needed only a good job to be self-sufficient and that he found soon after graduation. With a starting salary of $65 a week he was in good shape to be the "free agent" the agency was determined he should become. He felt no further need to lean on it for support and told Steingraph "most emphatically" that he was ready for his case to be closed. He felt he could manage quite well without the agency's "being in the picture" any longer.

Beggs and Cobb was a leather wholesaler and Mike would work in its Boston office for 42 years, his entire adult working life. He flourished in the stable working environment he found there. He grew fond of his colleagues as they did of him. Upon his death they honored him in particular for his patience, compassion and competence. By that time Mike had long since put his love for basketball, once an escape from responsibility, to extraordinarily good use as the inspiring coach of his younger daughter and hundreds of other teenage girls.

Mike and I had remained together, as our parents desired, for almost all of the twelve years of our association with the agency. Although I can't remember feeling anything of the sort at the time, and although we had already gone our separate ways, it strikes me now as fitting that we both should have ended our formal relationship with the agency at the same point in time: February of 1962. Thanks in large part to agency policy and practice we had become independent and self-assured young men ready and willing to take on what life had in store for us.

The tone of a letter I wrote to Herman Steingraph during the summer following my graduation from UMass seems to me to celebrate that readiness and my independence:

> Dear Mr. Steingraph:
>
> At the risk of boring you silly . . . I'll let you know what's been going on. Graduated, of course, from UMass on June 10 with a Cum Laud degree . . . and received a couple of other non-scholastic honors . . . Am working for The Wall Street Journal here in Dear ole Chicopee Falls . . . I plan to go to New York University part time next fall and will be going down this weekend to look around, look for a place to stay and for a job. Nothing else to let you in on. Hope to see you sometime before I go on my adventurous way.

I never did see him again.

BEATRICE CARTER MEETS MIETEK MOTYL

May 12, 1948

Traveler's Aid Desk,
South Station,
Boston, Mass.

This will introduce MIETEK MOTYL who is to go to the Jewish
Family & Children's Service, 6 North Russell Street, Boston.

We would appreciate it very much if you would place him in
a cab with instructions to the driver to take him to the
above address.

Lotte Marcuse
Director of Placements

MIETEK'S LETTER OF INTRODUCTION

Conclusion:
The Car Ride

You might say that this book began with a telephone conversation with Ellen Fishman, a social worker at the agency in Waltham, Mass. I called the agency in the hope of locating anyone who had been connected to it between 1950 and 1962, in the hope of making a start toward my distant goal. Everyone I talked to was supportive, even enthusiastic, but no one seemed to know who might help me find someone, anyone, who had shared my experience in any way. Finally I was directed to Ellen. Toward what seemed to be the end of another fruitless conversation she asked: "Does the name Leonard Serkess mean anything to you?" And here we are.

Len and I met after a hiatus of some fifty years in the company of our wives in the Serkess's Newton apartment. We talked for several hours before enjoying dinner at the nearby Marriott Hotel, on the site of Norumbega Park and the paddleboats I loved as a child. We have met several times since and have become friends. He directed me to others whom he thought might be helpful to me and who in turn might direct me to others, and so on. In this manner I have met many people who have contributed their experiences to this memoir.

When I lived in Bradshaw House one of our favorite activities was to go for a car ride. Several of us would pile into a housefather's car and just ride around and explore. Something like that is what Len suggested he and I do one fine spring day, but now with a specific goal in mind: to visit the buildings that had served as the study home, the Newton annex, and Bradshaw House, and then to visit my family's Seaver Street apartment building. We both wondered what had become of these buildings that had been witness to so much.

The annex, Beatrice Carter's house, was closest. The four of us climbed into Len's Chevy (though more decorously than did the children fifty years before) and drove the few miles to Circuit Road, just off Route 9. The cape had been a kind of overflow resource for the agency, and now I saw that it had become larger. I walked along the two streets that bordered its corner lot and thought that it could now house more children than it once did if the agency were still in the practice of child welfare. I took photographs and remembered the girl who lived down the street who threatened never to talk to me again if I persisted in squirting her with the garden hose. I remembered speeding down the hill on a bike with no brakes and crashing into the white picket fence across the street. I remembered Mrs. Carter and Miss Margolis standing patiently in the doorway while I and other boys ran wildly around the house. I remembered these and other things and when I rejoined my patient companions I was smiling broadly.

Len and I dropped off Suzanne and Sally at Boston's Fine Arts Museum and the two of us continued on. When we got to Brighton Center Len briefly became disoriented and I somehow managed to identify the street that would lead us directly to the home. Moving slowly down the tarred drive we could see that the building was inhabited—there were cars and mailboxes—and it soon became obvious that it had been divided into several apartment units. The two of us stood on the small landing to the locked side entrance and looked at each other.

Suddenly Len began vigorously pressing all of the buzzers by the door. He was determined to enter the building in which he had lived and worked with so many children during the early years of his first marriage. Someone, he thought, was bound to respond to his urgency and let him in.

I strolled about and took some pictures while Len waited for that response. But I couldn't find much to focus on until I entered what had been the front lawn and saw the white columns and broad steps of the gracefully curved portico, well maintained but apparently unused.

I returned to Len just in time to see the door open. A resident had unlocked it and she was willing to usher us in and talk to us once we had explained our conduct. But more meaningful to me than anything in our conversation was the central hall of the building, still dominated by the elegant staircase and the stained glass windows that accompanied anyone who mounted the stairs to the second floor. What must they have meant to the two boys who had been driven here by Leonard Serkess one dark night a lifetime away?

Smiling at the successful outcome of our rash behavior, we headed to Dorchester. Blue Hill Avenue looked as it always had, broad and inviting despite the absence of streetcar rails. Turning off the main thoroughfare, we had no problem finding the building that had once been Bradshaw House. It, too, had increased in size, at the expense of our dartboard and most of the side yard where the Bradshaw Bums had spent so much time. But it looked as if someone cared for it and it sported a fire escape on the front between the second and third floors that I didn't remember being there in 1953. And I thought of the story Robert Berger told me of climbing the internal stairs to the third floor and initiating his friendship with Shmulek with the offer of a glass of milk.

Bradshaw Street is part of a largely Black neighborhood today. I did not want to be seen by its residents as a suspicious person prowling about, so I resisted the temptation to walk along two sides of its corner lot as I had in Newton. I got out of the car, however, found an unobstructed view of the house, and took a photograph of its front. Then we were off to our final destination.

Seaver Street today is also part of a Black neighborhood but that does not explain my inability to get out of Len's car. He had parked in front of 132 and I looked about but remained seated. The empty lot where my friends and I had played ball and built our tree house had become a convenience store. The front of the apartment building had not changed and I remembered the way it looked just inside the front door where we tossed our waxed baseball cards against the wall beneath the mailboxes. When I glanced up the driveway that ran between the convenience store and the side of the building I could see the gray rectangle that I knew was the bathroom window of what had been our basement apartment, the window beside which my mother stood and tended to her face in the mirror. But I could not get out of the car to take that picture, nor the picture of the front entrance. Len asked if I wanted to take a picture and I said no and he waited for some moments and then we drove away.

Why could I not step out of the car and take those pictures?

Of all the sadness imbedded in my and Mike's case files, the early pages containing caseworkers' judgments of my mother's appearance and behavior were the most troubling to me. Often I sighed and closed the green loose-leaf binder in which I had organized the agency material and put it away, forcing myself to return sometime later. I read of my mother's bleach-blonde hair, her crooked teeth, her ill-fitting clothes, and the livid, exposed tissue of her right cheek. I read of her "desperate" attempts to ingratiate herself to others and of her "pathetic" ploys to be perceived as a literate and genteel woman. I read of her "compulsive" talking, of her "domineering" and "exacting" attitude toward those to whom she spoke and toward her children, in particular, whose future development, caseworkers feared, might be harmed by it. I read of this and more and my unspoken response was "No, that was not my mother. My mother was neither unattractive nor dangerous to me. That is not the mother I remember."

But there I was, in Leonard Serkess's car, *the* Mr. Serkess who recorded on November 1, 1950: "She is a rather unattractive woman . . . She definitely did not impress me as being a normal individual." There I was, in front of my family's home and burdened by judgments of my mother that were unknown to me as a child but that I am forced to confront today. I did not want to get any closer to 132 Seaver Street than I was to the disturbing information I had encountered in the green binder. I could not afford the sentimentality that required a photograph of the building's front door or of the kitchen windows I knew I would see if I walked up the driveway toward the bathroom window. I would stay in the car and leave that place.

Months after the trauma of that episode I recalled Dr. Platt's conclusion, garnered from his analysis of my psychological test results, that while "on the surface there seems to be little concern over the mother figure, projected testing suggests considerable anxiety over a non-nurturant mother image." Although in the process of writing this memoir I have painfully acquired a less "nurturant" impression of my mother than the one created by a child who avidly sought her love and care, I nevertheless cherish the contradictory image I retain and resist any opportunity to reduce its power. Frozen in Len's car, I had no strength to juxtapose the conflicting impressions I brought to my family's Roxbury address. Perhaps I feared what nearness to the actual shapes and spaces of my childhood there might induce me to accept. After all, this is *my mother* we are talking about.

As I now understand, it was the intensive observation and articulation by the very caseworkers who responded critically to my mother's appearance and behavior that moved the agency to make available to me and Mike a safe haven. These were skills that enabled caseworkers to monitor, to evaluate, to engage and finally to help the children for whom they were responsible. The sheer will and energy of Dora Margolis and Beatrice Carter to create a sophisticated casework service, the maintenance of high standards in the training and organization of casework personnel, the sensibility and professionalism of individual caseworkers—these critical elements and the funding that sustained them allowed the agency to care for me and Mike and many other children struggling within such various circumstances.

And so, rather than resenting those who punctiliously observed and evaluated my mother I am left with a deep sense of gratitude. When all is said, I can only marvel at the difference they made in the lives of children whose prospects without them and the institution they served were uninspiring.